I0486320

Trapped in Between:

Realities of the project world

Battles between the Boardroom
and the Project room

Ahmad Faisal PhD.

PMBOK® and PMP® are registered trademarks of Project Management Institute.

Library of congress cataloging – Publication Data
Faisal, Ahmad
     Trapped in between: Realities of the projects world / Ahmad Faisal p. cm.
Includes bibliographical references (p.   )

Note for Librarians: A cataloguing record for this book is available from Library and Archives Canada at www.collectionscanada.ca/amicus/index-e.html
ISBN 1-4251-0904-7

Offices in Canada, USA, Ireland and UK

Book sales for North America and international:
Trafford Publishing, 6E–2333 Government St.,
Victoria, BC V8T 4P4 CANADA
phone 250 383 6864 (toll-free 1 888 232 4444)
fax 250 383 6804; email to orders@trafford.com
Book sales in Europe:
Trafford Publishing (UK) Limited, 9 Park End Street, 2nd Floor
Oxford, UK OX1 1HH UNITED KINGDOM
phone +44 (0)1865 722 113 (local rate 0845 230 9601)
facsimile +44 (0)1865 722 868; info.uk@trafford.com
Order online at:
trafford.com/06-2662

10 9 8 7 6 5 4 3 2

In loving memory of my father, Mohd Hassan Bin Mohd Ali to whom I am forever indebted and may his soul is blessed.

Acknowledgement

Many hours were spent writing this book and thanks to modern technology, not many trees were cut, as today's word-processing software is extremely powerful. Knowledge is power meant to be shared amongst mankind, and not a "secret that one shall take to the grave". Hence, to those who seek knowledge for their betterment or that of their companies find this book of a value to them, I shall be very glad.

Thank you to all copyright holders for allowing me to use their materials. My sincere appreciation to all those who have made this book possible, my thanks to all my staff, my peers, my bosses, my project members, and other project team members for the experience. My deepest gratitude to my wife and kids for the support and encouragement; I could not have done it without you! I finally thank GOD for the knowledge and the blessings

GOD Bless us all

Preface

"Trapped in Between" is about the global realities in managing projects. It is about people trying to understand what makes their project work or makes it worse!

Many a time, we (myself included…) "cloud" our minds with symptoms and effects and fail to drive the issues at hand logically. Our reluctance to challenge the norms and not comprehend the actual situation has made us fail to bring issues to a common sense level.

We often make project decisions based on our opinions, which are primarily driven by our assumptions, the available information, and our inferences from past project experiences. Hence, we frequently observe many project decisions being made without prior understanding of the issues or using "half-baked" information generated by inaccurate data.

If you are nodding your head in agreement with my statements, congratulations. You've been there!

IF (the big IF… I must say), we clearly understand the situation at hand by asking the "right" people for the "right" information; half the battle is already won. The remaining half is merely to get everyone to do what they are supposed to do and do it well! By doing it right first time every time, we will set the project's journey on the right course.

This reminds me of what my father (may God bless his soul) used to say, *"Son, it is neither our job nor our position that we have to worry about, but our responsibilities…"* A short statement that contains deep meaning from a very wise man, but that is another story.

There are several reasons why I write in this manner. First, I want to make the project realities simple to understand. Second, I want to illustrate the relevancy of these realities to any project. Finally, is to prove that every one of us can be an outstanding project manager or be developed into one over time.

In this ever-changing business environment, organisations continuously try to improve their competitive position in the marketplace. In the excitement of such quests, organisations are bombarded with various change programs that have been developed, marketed, introduced, and implemented by various agencies, both locally and internationally. Program and Project Management is no exception. In fact, many times, the term project has been so *loosely* used to the extent that it has lost its real definition.

Rapid changes in both technology and the market place have created enormous strains on existing organisation's make up. Traditional structures that are highly bureaucratic can no longer respond fast enough to the continuously changing environments. This must be replaced by other temporary management organisation structures that are highly organic, fluidic, and responsive.

Project Management is not new! Although unsupported, the history of project management can be traced back to the ancient Egyptian era. Coupled with the advancement in management technology, project management has evolved into a more formal and structured management approach to implementing projects effectively and efficiently.

It was observed that, the acceptance of the project management approach has never been easy. The approach departs from the traditional business form that is functional, vertical, and hierarchical with a strong emphasis on the chain of command. This represents one of the many challenges to any project manager.

However, the biggest challenge that any project manager will face is the project itself. Orchestrating the total organisational effort in managing the interplay between the *technical, financial,* and *political* realities of any project demands significant effort.

I have seen project proposals that are technically sound yet rejected for implementation. Financial viability is often the basis for rejection. I can see that some of you are saying, *"That is the right thing to do!"*

Well, of course, I tend to agree with you on that. Unfortunately, technical and financial requirements most often do not work hand in hand, especially for projects in *service-oriented* industries.

Take a customer relationship program as an example. "I can see that many of those customer relationship management (CRM) consultants are arming themselves with flamethrowers to burn me, but hang on there and please allow me to finish…"

To exactly pin-down the return on investment or the internal rate of return for the proposed expenditure will require massive modelling and even with great success, the whole customer-value chain end-to-end processes need to be effective and efficient.

I agree that CRM may have contributed significantly, but the relationship is somehow correlational rather than causal. The success demands the whole customer-value chain machinery to perform like clockwork; *something that no one can promise!*

Hence, juggling the technical and financial realities can be a project manager's nightmare.

There is another reality in projects, which I was fortunate to observe and it represents the crux of my book. I have observed projects that are both technically sound and financially viable yet rejected for implementation. "I can sense that some of you are now frowning with a BIG question mark, WHY?"

I finally discovered that, although these projects were technically sound and financially viable, they were not *"politically correct"*.

Insufficient lobbying by the project manager or the project sponsors or the program director or whoever, has lead to poor buying-in by other stakeholders. The attacks on these projects were neither on technical nor on financial grounds, but purely on the acceptance of the project itself, that encroaches into other territories.

Some of you might view this scenario as failure by the project teams in getting the customers' acceptance or meeting the stakeholders' requirements. This is true from a certain point of view.

However, I would like to emphasise here that *"politically correct"* goes way beyond internal customers' acceptance or meeting stakeholders' requirements as it also concerns the covert agenda of certain individuals or groups that exist within any organisation. I have heard of cases where, despite the fact that it makes business sense to work with the proposed solution provider, projects have been rejected based on *"inappropriate"* provider selection.

So ladies and gentlemen, if you think that juggling projects based on them being just technically sound and financially viable is a nightmare, inclusion of the politically correct realities will make any project manager delusional!

About the book

May be you have come across books like this, or maybe not. Whichever the case may be, I consider this book as a *hybrid* blending the theories and the realities of the project world, literally!

There are chapters that you may find it to be theoretical as it is written as a thesis like a composition, especially the first few chapters. In other chapters, you may find it particularly interesting as they describe real life events. That is why I consider this book a hybrid as both the academicians and the practitioners can use it.

THIS BOOK IS NOT about high-level models and concepts in project management. I believe there are enough publications, books, and journals to discuss those issues. Although there are certain chapters or paragraphs that resemble a thesis, this was done intentionally to assist academicians and students alike in further research and citations.

THIS BOOK IS meant for those who wish to seek knowledge and understand the underlying *realities* that affect projects and project management as a whole. Individuals may, if they so wishes compare and contrast my findings with their own projects or organisation in manoeuvring their projects forward. This book also incorporates my research findings from 1988 to 2004 in both Malaysian as well as foreign companies that I have had close associations with.

About the author

Some of you might be sceptical about this book and some might even wonder whether it is worth reading. Here is something about myself. I am a Malaysian who did not get to go to a big college or major university for my first degree. Although I am a maintenance engineer by profession, I attended an apprenticeship program in Dublin, Eire on a full scholarship. Apprenticeship programs were popular back then for training a highly skilled workforce. They were not available in universities. They require the development of competencies with great emphasis on "hands-on" job experience.

I remember the first day when I was taught about housekeeping and the importance of keeping the workplace clean. That is a basic requirement of good maintenance engineering. I can still remember picking up a broom, sweeping the whole floor and my workbench to clear away debris that can be detrimental to critical components being worked on.

I was taught how to blend with a workforce of differing races, genders and ages; and how to be part of the production team. I mingled with the lower ranking staff on the production line - the engineering hands, helpers, fitters, mechanics, despatch clerks, and technicians; my peers the fellow engineers, my bosses the foremen, superintendents and managers. Trust and relationship building is of the utmost importance for workplace harmony and efficient workflow.

Upon graduation, I became a fully-fledged maintenance engineer.

After spending years as a maintenance engineer, I decided to get myself into the administration areas like production planning, support services, systems development and business development. That was when my project management involvement began and I became very passionate about it. Complementing my engineering qualifications, I attended part-time management programs, despite my hectic work schedule at my own expense.

Quenching my thirst for knowledge and experience, I moved away completely from the engineering environment. I stepped into the corporate world of marketing, customer and corporate services; while maintaining my passion for managing programs and projects, and taking up my part-time studies up to PhD, again at my own expense.

As you can see, I am not amongst those who are placed straight into the managerial group after completing their first degree. I started from the "pits" where the action was, moved myself into the cubicles of the complex labyrinth of departments and divisions; and later into my own cosy room with a secretary.

I have been on project assignments in Australia, Singapore, Indonesia, Hong Kong, Japan, China, United Kingdom, Germany, and United States of America. I have seen the worst and best of people and organisations, and have observed what people and organisations can do, for better or for worse.

After spending more than twenty years in change programs and project environments, and having conducted a longitudinal study over a period of sixteen years in the area of organisational change, program and project management, which happens to have been my doctoral thesis; I am in the opinion that I am ready to write this book.

A.F.

Contents

THE BASICS:
Projects, Project Management and Managing Projects

What are Projects, Project Management and Managing Projects?

I enjoy writing this part as I equate it to writing literature reviews and that is why I am writing it in a similar manner, to add value to academicians and students. Students doing their theses ought to be familiar with literature reviews, which I know they hate!

On many occasions, I was asked questions like, "Why are you specialising in this field?" some even asked me, "Why are you so passionate about project management?"

My brief response to them is that, "you have to understand what project and project management is all about, how it affects your life and only then will you understand my passion for this endeavour."

So what are projects, project management, and managing projects?

Project management discipline as well as its profession is gaining global popularity amongst many top organisations. The concept of project management or management by projects has enabled organisations to respond quickly and in a timely manner to the ever-changing competitive environment; and many organisations are using project management as part of their change programs or as the change agent itself.[1] Such an approach is being widely used in change programs as it allows organisations to collaborate cross-functionally like Boeing, BAT, Mobil, Rolls Royce and Sun Microsystem to cite a few. This is due to its uniqueness and the inherent advantages project management possesses[2].

---

[1] Adizes, 1988, Atkinson, 1990; Block, 1999; Block and Frame, 1998; Bryde, 2002; 2003; Cicmil, 2000; Ohmae, 1991; Pitagorsky, (n.d) and Smith & Dodds, 2001.
[2] Kerzner, 1992.

Change is inevitable! The rate of change varies with the industry, and the sources of change are multi-faceted. Organisation must embrace change. They have to learn and adapt to these changes or be prepared to accept a fate similar to the dinosaurs and other pre-historic creatures[3]. Since managing change and uncertainty is a continuous endeavour in any organisation, issues facing project management can be considered as current and remain relevant in the current and future business environment of any organisation.

However, more often than not, the project management approach has been frequently applied without any real understanding of its appropriateness within the overall organisational fit. Hence, when projects within the total program are not up to expectations, project management has been frequently blamed.

There are various views when it comes to the definition and expansion of the term *project* and *project management.*

Concise Oxford English dictionary (2002: page 1143) defines project as an enterprise carefully planned to achieve a particular aim, a proposed or planned undertaking.

Pinto and Slevin (as cited in Cleland & King, 1988: page 481) provides a definition of a project as an organisation of people dedicated to a specific purpose or objective. Projects generally involve large, expensive, unique, or high-risk undertakings, which have to be completed by a certain date, for a certain amount of money, within some, expected level of performance. At a minimum, all projects need to have well defined objectives and sufficient resources to carry out the entire required task.

Kerzner (1992: page 2) defines a project as any series of activities and tasks that have specific objectives to be completed within certain specifications, have a defined start and end date, have funding limitations and consume resources.

---

[3] Ohare, 1988; Peter, 1989.

Kepner and Tregoe (as cited in Ahmad Faisal (1992)(a)) defines a project as a series of interrelated activities undertaken to accomplish a specific goal or end result. A project has a specific start and finish; it is not ongoing.

Cleland and King (1983: pages 70-73) defines a project as a complex effort to achieve a specific objective within a schedule and budget target, which typically cuts across organisational lines, is unique and is usually not repetitive within the organisation. The project is not a permanent entity but, rather, an activity whose purpose is to work itself into dissolution after the objectives of the project have been accomplished. These objectives are threefold: to accomplish the project on schedule, within budget and with its technical objectives achieved.

Project Management Body of Knowledge or more widely known as, **PMBOK®** in both **1996** and **2000 editions (page 4)** defines a project in terms of its distinctive characteristics; a project is a temporary endeavour undertaken to create a unique product or service. Temporary means that every project has a definite beginning and end. Unique means that the product or services are different in some distinguishing way from all other products or services. Projects are a means to respond to those requests that cannot be addressed within the organisation's normal operational limit.

Turner and Cochrane (as cited in Cicmil, 1999; Lee-Kelly, 2002) defines project as: an endeavour in which human, material and financial resources are organised in a novel way, to undertake a unique scope of work of given specification, within constraints of cost and time, so as to achieve unitary, beneficial change, through the delivery of quantitative and qualitative objectives.

Gouse and Stickney (as cited in Cleland & King, 1988: page 870) defines project management as the application of the systems approach to the management of technologically complex tasks or projects whose objectives are explicitly stated in terms of time, cost and performance parameters.

Kerzner (1990: page 18) defines project management as the process of achieving project objectives through the traditional organisational structure and the specialities of the individuals concerned.

Kerzner (1992: pages 4-6) provides an overview definition of project management as the planning, organising, directing and controlling of company's resources for a relatively short-term objective that has been established to achieve specific goals and objectives. Furthermore, project management utilises the systems approach to management by having functional personnel (vertical hierarchy) assigned to a specific project (the horizontal hierarchy). The short-term objective is qualified by variations in the industries. Since project deliverables must serve specific needs of customers, the project must be managed within good customer relations.

Kepner and Tregoe (as cited by Ahmad Faisal (1992)(a)) defines project management as the actions taken to define the project's requirements; plan the activities to accomplish the requirements; and ensure successful project implementation.

Badiru (as cited in Badiru & Pulat, 1995: page 2) initially defines project management as the process of managing, allocating, and timing resources to achieve a specific goal in an efficient and expedient manner. On the same premise, **Badiru and Pulat (1995: page 2)** has expanded the definition of project management as the systematic integration of technical, human, and financial resources to achieve goals and objectives.

PMBOK® (1996: page 6) defines project management as the application of knowledge, skill, tools, and techniques to project activities in order to meet or exceed stakeholders' need and expectations from a project. In the **2000 edition (page 6)**, it was revised to the application of knowledge, skill, tools, and techniques to project activities to meet project requirements. Project management is accomplished using the processes such as initiating, planning, executing, controlling, and closing.

Drucker (1988: pages 11-33) viewed management from the tasks, responsibilities, and practices of a manager. The scientific theory talks about management from what a manager does such as planning, organising, staffing, directing, controlling, reporting, and budgeting while the behavioural theory talks about management from the people's perspective such as motivation, ethics, and values.

Cicmil (1997) stated that there has been a shift in many organisations in applying project management practices to certain critical business operations or key processes. The practice of *"projectising"* critical business operations has taken the discipline beyond the traditional project management approach. There is an emerging trend regarding broader application of project management in organisations. It is believed that the theory and practices of project management have fundamentally changed over the past decade. Traditionally, project management is being applied to manage unique, capital intensive, non-operational activities in project-based industry such as construction, engineering, and defence. However, emergent project management is now being applied in a broader perspective as a tool for managing all types of change initiatives within all types of organisations. There was also emphasis on both upstream activities, such as aligning the projects with the organisation's strategy and defining stakeholders' requirements; and downstream activities such as performance review and lessons learnt[4].

In summing up it can be seen that definition of project and project management centred on similar keywords.

Therefore, a **Project** can be considered as; a temporary undertaking that contains a series of inter-related activities that are to be completed within a specific time, a specific budget, and meeting specific performance levels (agreed requirements and expectations).

---

[4] Bryde, 2003; Prasad, 1995.

Project Management on the other hand, can be viewed from two perspectives. One is about an undertaking, from the *process perspective*, and the other, from the *managerial perspective*. What these definitions have in common is about using *people* within the organisation to carry out the processes and managing them in the most effective and efficient manner.

Therefore, **Project Management** is the application of knowledge, skill, tools, and techniques to project activities to meet project requirements; and **Managing Projects** is about the 'art and science of getting the project done with and through people'.

Supported by my own research, it shows that, seventy eight percent (78%) of project success or failure evolves around managerial issues such as management support and leadership. Hence, the phrase, "take care of the people and the project will take care by itself" was born.

In simple terms, a project is about getting to do something within sets of constraints (*scope, time, money,* and *needs* or *expectations*), and project management and managing projects is about planning, organising, budgeting, directing and reporting the activities that are required to be done with and through people.

However, despite the numerous research and development studies conducted on managerial issues, there is still too much emphasis placed on project management methodologies, processes, and tools. Please remember that, these are merely tools to assist you and do not replace YOU as the project mover!

The demand for managerial and leadership competencies is far greater that the tools themselves, in manoeuvring and delivering the project outcome.

Opening up the Space:

Opening my inner space and amplifying my brief answer to most frequently asked questions.

"Why are you specialising in this field?"

"Why are you so passionate about program and project management?"

On many occasions, the above questions were asked of me, and my brief response to them is that, "you have to understand what project and project management is all about, how it affects your life and only then will you understand my passion for this endeavour."

I believe that project management touches every aspect of our lives. Looking at the definition expounded earlier, project management revolves around both our personal and professional activities.

At the work place, we are assigned to either head a project or as part of a project team. We are expected to be good team players supporting the project's goals and objectives. Likewise, we are also expected to collectively share the responsibilities to deliver the project's outcomes and be rewarded once the project is successfully closed-out.

In our personal lives, going off for a holiday trip can be considered a project. If you are a Malaysian citizen and planning for a holiday trip, say to the US with your family, there is a lot of pre-planning that needs to be done: making the travel and accommodation arrangements; making sure your travel documents are in order and obtaining a visa from the US Embassy; ensure there are enough funds to cover all essential expenses with a certain percentage for contingencies: loosing your baggage, flight delays, falling sick in a foreign land and etc. And this does not take into account the amount of money required for leisure and shopping expenses. Shopping at Tiffany can burn a hole in your pocket!

You can see that managing the activities for your holiday trip is like managing a project. It has specific scope: you are governed by the rules and regulation of originating and destination country. It has specific start and end dates. It needs to be funded, and there are needs and expectations attached to the particular trip like a visit to Disney World, driving through Sunset Boulevard and shopping for souvenirs or personal items.

Publishing this book is also a project on its own. It has all the elements of a project, by definition. This book started with an idea, conceptualising the topic and the messages to be put across. In a project sense, this is building the scope for the book. It is critical, as I do not want to stray from the key points. I also have to remain focused on what my readers' expectations are whilst not breaking any laws governing such publications. There then followed all the necessary activities to complete "the project": planning the outline, literature reviews, building the manuscript, proof reading, printing and finally we have the published product; the one that you are now reading.

Looking at the definition of project and project management, if you think about it, life itself is one big complex program with numerous projects and sub-projects within it.

In every life, we have a start date, that is your date of birth and it comes complete with the place and time of birth as well! It is just that the end date remains unknown but we all know that we will depart one day.

We live within the scope or boundaries that exist within our societal and cultural norms. Although to some, growing up is a process, it is a project on its own. We need to fund our growth and of course, our parents or our legal guardians were the ones playing the role of the project manager and financiers during our early childhood.

As we step into colleges and universities, we now slowly take over the role of the project manager. We begin to carve out our mission, goals and setting targets for our CGPA. We seek scholarships to finance our studies and at times apply for grants to fund our research projects. After graduation, we step into the real world of work and project assignments. Only to discover that it is a life, full of surprises that were never taught in classrooms.

Welcome to the *realities* of the project world and YOU are on your own!

The next phase is where your life's project becomes more challenging and more complicated. You now start having your own place, your own car, and your own joint where everybody knows your name. This reminds me of my favourite TV series in the eighties, "Cheers".

When you are at certain age, your parents will be asking the question that you wished they had never asked.

The one million dollar question, *"When are you getting married?"*

However, if you were to analyse your parents' intent, the question is not so much about you. More often that not, it is they (your parents) who are at the stage of craving for grandchildren! It is a circle of life. Should you decide to take the wedding vows and start your own family, you will be looped into the same circle sooner than you thought possible!

So make no mistake about it, project management touches every aspect of our lives, whether *professionally* or *personally*. Hence, how can I not be passionate about it?

SUCCESS FACTORS:
What make a project successful or otherwise?

What are Success, CSF and KSF?

I have attended numerous project proposal briefings; project presentations, seminars, workshops and plenary sessions moderated by experts (project management consultants and practitioners). I have heard these experts preach about project success and the importance of managing a project's critical success factors in moving forward. I have also heard terms like key success factors being used by these experts on the same platforms.

The irony is that the way a project's key success factors (**KSF**) are explained, sounds similar to of those the project's critical success factors (**CSF**). Are they the same or different?

In answering the question, let us review the keywords used.

What is Project Success?

Project success is when the outcome of a particular undertaking *primarily* meets the customers' requirements and expectations and *secondarily*, is completed within the agreed timeframe and within the approved budget. Requirements are those documented attributes the product or services (outcome of the project) must have or provide, and expectations are those non-documented attributes the product or services (outcome of the project) are able to provide. Once these are met, a project is considered as successful.

You must be asking how I arrive at such an opinion. The following represents a view based on extensive literature reviews and my project experience.

Regardless of what other literature has got to say on this, projects will not be successful if we are not clear on what success is. Therefore, it is important for us to be clear about what success is and understand the rules associated with project success. In my opinion, there are just *two* rules to project success. The *first rule*: project success has to be defined, well articulated, adequately communicated, and agreed and the *second rule*: project success has to be meaningfully measured against what has been defined and agreed.

Here, I will use the thesis writing manner to give due respect to authors that have conducted research and contributed to the discipline of project management.

Rule No.1: Defining Project Success

Success means different things to different people. It is due to the subjective nature of human mind in target setting, that is why I set the first rule as: Success has to be *defined*, well articulated, adequately communicated, and agreed.

In any performance management literature that you may have come across, a great deal of emphasis is placed on performance planning such as conducting a business purpose analysis, process validation and alignment, setting the business goals and objectives and so on and so forth.

By defining the project success, we are able to establish the *parameters* for sentencing project success in entirety or in parts.

It has to be understood that, the success of projects is not binary; they do not simply succeed or fail. Any useful project has a range of processes and outcomes. These may be thought of as targets that are achieved more or less successfully. Hence, before a project commences, there should be agreement on how achievement of particular targets or objectives will be measured, and this should be specified. The relative importance of the different targets should be agreed and specified to provide a means of weighing partial success when some objectives are met[5].

---

[5] Allgar, Heywood, Lesse, and Walker, 2001.

Empirical evidence in recent years has illuminated a delicate issue of differentiating between project goals (the ultimate benefit or purpose of the project) and delivery objectives (the outcome or product of project effort according to the specifications, within time and cost constraints). There has been little understanding of the dynamic link between these two. Given the specific, visionary nature of goals and desired strategic benefits of change projects, these factors present the gaps in the management and implementation of change projects because of the inherent difficulties in their precise interpretation and definition from the start. This implies that particular attention, effort, inspiration, and creativity are required from change leaders and project managers to define the methods, and communicate and negotiate the objectives with the rest of the organisation[6].

Hence, the need to define project success is imperative.

RULE NO.2: MEANINGFUL MEASURES

Measuring does not mean that we can "pick and choose" any items from the "basket of measures" in attempting to fill up the measurement scorecard. It has to be *meaningful*. We must be able to use these measures as indicators, for us to *control* the project's progress and manage any deviations. I emphasise the word control here as I have frequently observed project teams attempting to measure items that are beyond their control. This I consider as meaningless!

The axiom, "what gets measured gets done" can be viewed similarly as "what can be measured can be controlled", only the applicability and extent of control varies. That is why project managers are advised to carefully seek out measurements that are within their control.

The second rule proposes that project success has to be *meaningfully measured* against what success has been defined and agreed.

---

6 Cicmil, 1999

It has been noted in various researches that change projects fail due to inadequate attention being given to the role played by measurement. The use of numbers allows organisations to create awareness, publicise, and motivate the project's stakeholders towards achieving the desired project results. Likewise, "hard data" does assist organisations to de-politicise what can be considered politically sensitive and allows organisations to learn from what went wrong and what was done right. Hence, well-defined measurement processes, measuring the correct measure must be put in place for projects to succeed[7].

Unfortunately, there is no one-measurement process that fits all. Nevertheless, this does not make a measurement system less important. Although projects may technically be similar, measuring success for a five-year research and development (R&D) project will differ from a three-year capital acquisition project, which is also different from a one-year process improvement project. The primary difference between failure and success is that, a successful project creates value that addresses the obvious challenges associated with what the project set out to do[8].

So, what would make a meaningful measure?

There has been a shift towards adopting customers' or stakeholders' acceptance as a key measure. In my opinion, it makes good sense. After all, ALL project outcomes are to serve a purpose set by their customers and stakeholders.

Let us re-visit the CRM project that I have cited earlier. Assuming that, the project team was able to deliver all the technical requirements within the specified budget and timeframe, this can be considered as successful at the project level. However, due to process breakages and other problems occurring within the customer-value chain, the company was not able to gain the full benefit from such implementation. To sanction the project as a failure on such a basis can be misleading.

---

[7] Hacker and Washington, 2004; Nemati and Barko, 2003.
[8] Edwards and Ewen, 1996; Suomala and Jokioinen, 2003;

It has to be understood that there is a distinction between *project performance* (that exclusively measures time, cost, and specifications) and *project management performance* (that looks into the multi-dimensional, multiple stakeholders, and quality of processes as well as product paradigm) for defining success. Although the two are inter-linked, they are different and it is important not to confuse the two[9].

However, the agreement for one common body of knowledge in the field of project management worldwide is yet to be reached and there has been disparity in project scheduling literature in terms of project problems commonly studied versus the problems in practice. Various studies have indicated that measuring the customers' acceptance is the most likely way forward in measuring project success and have shown that customer focus holds regardless of type of project and industry classification. Measuring customers' or stakeholders' acceptance has also been found to be put into practice without many difficulties[10].

It is then obvious that, without proper definition of success and not measuring success meaningfully can be disastrous for any project or organisation.

In summing up, the term *success* carries various meanings depending on the author's perspective. However, based on the literature and on observations, project success is when the outcome of a particular undertaking primarily meets the customers' requirements and expectations and secondarily, is completed within the agreed timeframe and within the approved budget, as how I have described it earlier.

---

[9] Bryde, 2003; Stewart, 2001.
[10] Kuruppuarachchi, Mandal and Smith, 2002; Meredith and Mantel (1995) as cited in Hides and Irani, 2000; Morris, 2001;Tukel and Rom, 2001.

What are CSF and KSF?

Critical success factors (CSF), are factor that have a *decisive importance* in the success or failure of projects, while **Key success factors** (KSF), are factors that have a *significant influence* on the CSF and project's outcome. This can be best illustrated graphically as shown below.

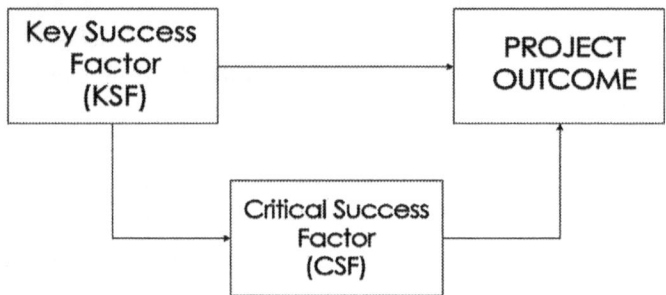

In forming the above opinion on CSF and KSF, please allow me to share with you some of the observations made during my project involvement and where necessary I will cite contributions made by other authors in the field of project management.

THE SITUATION

In most of the literature that I have reviewed and based on inputs given by many program or project management practitioners that I have met, top management support or management support or executive support is the number one hit on the success factors' list.

The question put forward to them and even to myself sometimes, "if management support is the most critical success factor, why is it project success is still far from desired?" After all, most of the major in-company programs or projects are presented to the senior management (board inclusive) and will not proceed without their approval and blessing! This, I consider as a *challenge* to all these project success problems that we are facing. Most of the so-called experts that I have met puzzle over my statement and grinned.

Now the next question is, "if management support is critical, what factor(s) influence senior management (board inclusive) to behave in a certain manner to a particular program or project?" and "What drives them to full throttle in supporting the projects or vice-versa?"

Armed with this set of questions, I set out on a journey into the unknown and it took me years to find the unknown. Please allow me to share with you the findings of my quest.

Being involved in numerous projects across numbers of companies worldwide, I was amused to find out a *peculiar behaviour* at certain levels in the management group. When faced with programs or project failures, the favourite question asked was, "what is causing these project failures?" Well, it is quite typical I guess.

However, I have also lived long enough to discover that the answer to such a question was also typical across the board, and it seems to be a favourite one as well. The answer was, "Project management competency is very much lacking within the organisation".

Then, the next question asked, "if project management competency is the cause to all these failures, why aren't the project teams being developed in these competencies?"

This round of questioning will continue until someone or something takes the fall for such failures.

Such phenomena, which I term as *"the circus of project failures"* is quite a performance!

I thought I was being paranoid, thinking that the above observations were purely mine and there was something seriously wrong with me! It haunted me for years until, when I was requested to present a paper on project management at an international conference. My paper received a tremendous response and during my post-presentation discussions, I discovered that "the circus of project failures" is performing worldwide!

You would not believe how relieved I was to have made such an important discovery. I was cured of something that I did not suffer from in the first place!

During my involvement as a program director, project manager or project team member or project facilitator or a trainer in the field of project management, I have observed that, there was an apparent lack of understanding on project management knowledge and its associated success factors. These were prevalent across various project teams and their performing organisations. Consequently, this has hindered smooth project implementations.

PROJECT OWNERS DISCUSSIONS

Without going into too many details of my quest, suffice to say that during the course of various projects, individual project owners were informally interviewed using a structured set of questionnaires to solicit their input as well as feedback on their projects.

Since it was informally done, the project owners were more relaxed and more receptive to the line of questions that I asked. My aim was to determine what in their opinion are factors that influence their projects and what other factors influence their (project owners) actions and behaviours in relation to project support and success.

My discussions with all the project owners and project sponsors revealed some interesting findings.

Project sponsors or project owners holds senior positions within the company. Some do have much experience in running their operations while some do not. These project sponsors or owners do subscribe to the concept of team building and cross-functional collaboration. However, further in-depth discussions reveal that the "know-how" in managing such processes is very much lacking and was left largely to the appointed project managers.

In most of the non-project based companies that I came across, the drive towards having specific project management policies, procedures, and processes was almost non-existent. I presume that it was such, as a project management set up was not part of their core business. Hence, it was left to the appointed consultants (if any), project managers, and the project teams to figure out the details. Meaning to say, only a handful of individuals have a clue about what and where the project is heading.

Concerning the project's critical success factors, results of my discussions reveals that forty percent (40%) of the project owners placed their emphasis on project management competency. Thirty-one percent (31%) placed their emphasis on project management infrastructure (such as organisation structure, systems, people and processes) to support their projects while twenty nine percent (29%) placed their emphasis on top management support for the projects. Please allow me (**AF**) to share with you some of the extracts from the project owners' (**PO**) discussions.

AF: "Top management support?" (I asked again just to be sure that I heard them right).

PO: "Yes! Even we, the project owners who sit in senior positions, still need the support from the above". (While pointing their fingers towards the boardroom direction).

AF: "How about the project manager appointment and team member selection?"

PO: "well, usually the proposal will put forward a few names and after much deliberation, we collectively agree, that the project manager must be appointed from the area that will be most likely affected by the project outcome". (Taking a short breath and continues) "We also agree that the project team members should comprise members from various areas that have a stake in the project".

AF: "I believe that this is a normal and common practice anywhere".

My observations show that the majority of project personnel, though some have worked in projects before, have neither being scheduled for nor attended a proper project management development program. Hence, project effectiveness and efficiencies were being questioned frequently.

AF: "What do you think about management levels attending some sort of project management development program?"

PO: "well, these sorts of programs are more relevant to the working teams themselves as we understand the project perfectly well and we know how to go about doing it".

Their responses were very much skewed towards denial of such needs. This was contrary to my discussions with the project team members. Project teams insisted that project owners have to undergo some kind of project management development training prior to giving the go-ahead to any major project. *"Escalated issues that require decisions from the project owners were left to the last minute and crisis management was the predominant practice!"* the project teams claimed.

I guess that is why many of the project managers that I have met suffer from hypertension, gastritis or some other kind of health disorder. The lack of knowledge and understanding of project management amongst the project owners in itself is enough to kill a good project manager!

Many programs and projects were running concurrently within the organisation and typically, all projects were going after the same pool of resources, both human and non-human resources. When I asked the project owners how they generally prioritise these projects, their responses shed more interesting findings.

PO: "We gave due considerations to those projects that, one (selecting his first finger), have a direct impact to the business goals and or two (selecting the second finger), the organisation was requested to participate in."

Of course, wanting to know more, I sought further clarification of their statements.

AF: (puzzled) "I'm clear on point number one, but how about point number two?"

I could sense some reluctance on their part. However, they were kind enough reply.

PO: "well, sometimes, being a high profile company, we are requested to carry out some projects under the umbrella of national service or social obligations" (ending the answer with a cynical smile).

Their voice tone and facial expressions told me not to probe further. Acknowledging that, I sought their permission before proceeding with my next question and they nodded in agreement.

AF: "How do you determine your level of involvement in a particular project?"

PO: "Gosh, you sure know how to load a riffle don't you?" (Smiling in response, trying to duck the question).

AF: (I remained calm and smiled back).

PO: "Concerning our level of support and involvements, it depends on the priority, meaning the visibility of the projects". (I frowned as they continued). "If a project is being discussed frequently, like an agenda at management meetings or board meetings, or even in the executive lounge, we better have the facts at our finger tips, or else, we are toasted!" (and we laughed).

Amidst the laughter, I could detect that there were some underlying messages they wanted to put across. Seeing the mood was good, I quickly interjected with another question seeking more clarification.

AF: "Would you be kind to elaborate on the visibility of project?"

PO: "You see, any projects have the "political" aspect of it. Project politics is something implied rather than outwardly stated. We use the safer term "project visibility" to describe project politics and nobody gets upset, right?"

AF: (nodded in agreement), "err... yes, I guess so, and being in your position, you would surely know better".

My reply may have sounded like "buttering", but I admired their creativity in selecting the terms used, and I have to give them credit for that!

It would appear therefore, that the higher the visibility, the higher is the need to close out the projects successfully. This would translate into a higher level of top management involvement and support.

PROJECT TEAM DISCUSSIONS

At the same time, I also took the liberty of discussing projects and project management issues with the project team members. During all my project involvements, I like to break the members into two separate groups and ask them questions unique to each group. I asked one team to list ten (10) most critical factors that would *make their project successful* while the other, to list ten (10) most critical factors that would *make their project fail.*

Now you see why I have to break them into two separate groups. Else, they might just reverse the list of the other and will remove the fun out of it, isn't it?

True enough, when these groups converged, the list of ten (10) most critical factors put forward by both groups was found to be on a similar note.

In summarising the list, it can be concluded that managerial issues such as setting project direction, managing project teams and leadership accounted for seventy eight percent (78%) of the project success or failures; sixteen percent (16%) was attributed to the project's technical glitches; and six percent (6%) was due to the changes in the business environment. When opened for discussions, all the project team members were in agreement with their findings.

Please allow me to share with you some of the extracts made from the team (**PT**) discussions.

AF: "Would anyone elaborate on project directions and leadership?"

PT: "We were just like lost souls wondering about as none of the owners actually know where we are heading."

I was stunned with such response and probed further about the owners' presence in projects meetings.

AF: "What about the owners' presence at project meetings?"

PT: "We hardly see their faces and our meeting invitations were frequently declined".

AF: "So how do you provide or receive feedback on what's happening in the company that may affect your project?"

PT: (hastily responded), "emails, what else!" (and continued), "We do see them face to face though, when they (owners) are in trouble!"

I know it was mischievous of me, but when I sensed that there was much resentment within the team members, I fired up with more questions, charging up the mean probing streak in me.

AF: "How then do you get the decisions made on your project issues or problems?"

Their response was overwhelming. I had opened up a Pandora's Box! The predominant response was:

PT: "They (the owners) don't have a clue as to what they want us to do, and most of the time they were asking the impossible!"

AF: "I believe that these are common grouses from all project teams, as I have heard them much too often".

PT: "They (the owners) deny that there is a problem until it is slapped right in front of their faces!" (Not satisfied with this remark, the team mentioned further), "Just because they sleep on the problem, we end up with sleepless nights correcting the situation."

I was really having a fun time getting the uncensored versions of what is actually happening to the project from the team members themselves. I asked the team members:

AF: "Why do you place changes to the environment (business or otherwise) as one of the success factor?"

PT: "We do understand why certain projects gets shelved due to factors such as economic crises, changes in the foreign exchange rates, 9/11, epidemic like SARs and other natural disasters such as earthquakes or Tsunami". (Empathising with the project owners and the management as a whole), "These are something beyond us and we can't do much about it".

However, something that the team added which attracted my attention,

PT: "But what we don't understand is that, too frequent changes in ownership and management structure have created tremendous pressure on the project and the team!" (Expressing their frustrations).

This relates back to my discussions with the project owners concerning their level of support and involvement. Since management support and involvement relates to the project's politics, also known as project's visibility, changes of guards and ownership may have changed some of the projects' priorities and demands.

During the team members' discussions, I also asked them about their level of exposures to projects and project management training or development programs. Although some of the members claimed that they have been involved in projects before, none had been scheduled for a proper project management program. "We were just expected do the project within an unrealistic deadline!" they claimed.

The team members also collectively agreed that, "They (the owners) must attend some form of workshop on managing projects and only then start managing us as a project team!"

The project teams admitted that they had encountered a number of 'bad' decisions made by their owners and this had hampered progress, disillusioned team members and project deadlines became moving targets.

In summary, we are now able to discern a salient factor affecting a project's success. This factor evolves around *top management support* and *project politics* or safely termed project visibility.

Determining CSF and KSF

So, what constitute *critical* success factors and what constitute *key* success factors?

Let us review what other authors or practitioners have to say on this important aspect of managing projects. We shall then link it back to the contents of my discussions with the project owners and project team members and placed it in a proper context.

CSF: MANAGEMENT SUPPORT

From preceding input, we see the need for a broader understanding of critical factors influencing project outcomes. These factors present themselves as 'multi-faceted' thus requiring multiple perspective views brought about by the 'multiple realities' of the business world[11].

Research has shown widespread agreement that project leadership is the number one enabling factor that drives a project through. It is central to both 'hard' and 'soft' issues pertaining to projects. Within the domain of technical project management, researchers now recognise that technology is more a secondary issue. Leadership and congruence of the team, make up major factors in team performance and project success. Empirical testing within case studies has also shown that senior management commitment and development needs of senior directors, amongst others are critical for change success. Lack of top management support through poor leadership has made it difficult for projects to pull through and created many pressures on the project teams[12].

Kuruppuarachchi, Mandal and Smith (2002) conducted a critical review on seventeen (17) critical success factors (CSF) advocated by eight (8) authors in the field of project management knowledge. Through the comparative study, it provides an insight as to what is the general theme for all these CSF.

Further in-depth analysis of the CSF reveals that nine (9) of those seventeen (17) factors are purely relating to managerial issues. This represents fifty three percent (53%) of the success factors. Although the remaining eight (8) factors are debatable, it can be seen that through active involvement and effective intervention by top management, it will greatly solves or facilitate most of the remaining factors. Taking all these into considerations, it can be safely deduced that high-level involvement by top management is critical to project success.

---

[11] Cicmil, 2000; David, 1987; DeBono, 1989 and Herzog, 2001.

[12] Bryde, 2002; Hacker and Washington, 2004; Haikonen, Savolainen and Ja¨rvinen, 2003; Henderson and McAdam, 2000; Hides and Irani, 2000; Jiang, Klien and Chen, 2001; Loo, 1996; Nemati and Barko, 2003; Oldenboom and Abratt, 2000; Sivakumar and Nakata, 2003; Sotiriou and Wittmer, 2001 and Thite, 1999.

Since a project's success is closely linked to visible support from the senior management and the owners throughout the project, the role of the owners is pivotal. They should be well versed in developing support for the project, protecting project commitments from other organisational priorities and demonstrating continued support for the effort in ways visible to all the project stakeholders. Teamwork at all levels of an organisation is also important to encourage innovation and radical improvement[13].

Surveys conducted by Standish Group International Inc. indicated that executive support, that used to be on the second order of importance in the year 1995, has moved up to the number one spot in the year 2001[14].

The field of project management is never short of critical success factors (CSF) advocated by various authors and practitioners. The most common CSF quoted in various literatures pointed to the works of **Pinto and Slevin, 1987 as cited in Cleland and King, 1988** that includes *management support* as one of the CSF.

Basing on the project team discussions, seventy-eight percent (78%) of project success or failures evolve around managerial issues that point to management support. Project owners on the other hand are of the opinion that only twenty nine percent (29%) of project success is attributed to management support for the projects. Even though the intensity of such factor varies between the two groups, both parties acknowledged the criticality of top management support to project success.

Here, management support refers to the level of involvement by project owners, project sponsors, management team, and board members in a particular project. This is attributed to their leadership style and context, setting and steering project directions, defending commitments made in the project and making available the necessary resources for the projects to succeed. Since management support has a *decisive importance for project success*, therefore, *management support is considered as the critical success factor*.

---

[13] Chu, 1997; Cicmil, 1999; Drew, 1996; Groberg and Riskas (n.d); Seely and Duong, 2001; Smith, 2003; Stebbin, Shani, Moon and Bowles, 1998; Whittaker, 1999; Zhang and Doll, 2001.
[14] The Chaos, 1995 and The Extreme Chaos, 2001.

KSF: PROJECT VISIBILITY A.K.A PROJECT POLITICS

If you recall our earlier discussion with the project owners, it was noted that the level of support by top management is depended upon the extent of their required involvement that is based on the *project's visibility*, which is a safer way of describing the *project politics*. This goes to say, the higher the visibility, the higher is the need to close out the projects successfully that translates into higher level of top management involvement.

Let us discuss on project visibility and see how visibility affects top management involvement and support.

Projects and project management do not occur in a vacuum. It requires an infusion of enthusiasm and commitment from various project stakeholders. The key for project success is how and when to 'connect' to the organisational grid through key connectors that is, the appropriate stakeholders. Without attention to various stakeholders' needs and expectations, projects will not be regarded as successful even if they were completed on time, within budget and specifications. Projects are affected by both the hidden agenda and the overt actions of people or groups. These groups extend well beyond the recognised traditional stakeholders. In large complex organisations, understanding the power structures and using them to influence project outcomes are often understood as politics. Project politics represents the actions and interactions between project team members and people outside the team that have impact on the overall success of the project[15].

It is also worth noting that politics is an influencing process (positive or negative) depending on whether one's cognitive map is being threatened or supported. Behaviours that are acceptable are a particular set of behaviours that fits the cognitive map of the incumbent[16].

---

[15] Bourne and Walker 2004.
[16] Peters, 1987.

Benefits or threats of change programs and its associated projects are perceived differently in different organisational unit and at different levels of hierarchy. One basic assumption in the concept of organisational change is that those concerned or affected obtained advantages from co-operations towards change. The provision of payoffs for the team is an important reason for co-operative behaviour. In organisational units, the interest cannot be seen homogeneously pro or contra to a change but can be different depending on the top management subjective perspective and anticipation of cost and benefits according to their interest. These political pressures will shape the behaviour towards the project[17].

Since projects are likely to effect change, change projects are not the final solution but rather a temporary equilibrium in an on-going contest between groups, each seeking to promote its own interest. This has affected the attention to the interests of those promoting particular objectives of the projects and to the interests of those opposing it. Groups may embed social controls within the application of projects while masking their motives with rhetoric's about improvements and efficiency. Therefore, these political forces (for or against) acting on these projects have to be acknowledged. These forces need to be explicitly managed since they contribute to an important part of the project success; and neglecting these forces often underlies disappointments of stakeholders' expectations[18].

Cultural factors were observed to have an impact on change projects as well. Hence, it is important to take these factors at both societal and organisational levels into consideration when drawing conclusions. Change projects can have unexpected and unintended consequences for reasons that are rooted in societal and organisational values and norms[19].

Although there has not been much research done on project visibility per se, it can be safely deduced that there are a number of influencing factors that affect how projects are being viewed by the various stakeholders.

---

[17] Strehl and Hugh, 1997.
[18] Boudreau and Robey, 1996.
[19] Carnall, 1991; Davis, 1987; Davison and Martinsons, 2002; Handy, 1987; 1990; Luthans, 1989; and Rashid, Sambasivan and Rahman, 2004.

Hence, the prioritisation of certain projects and the levels of management support take into account the political influence acting from both outside as well as within the project itself.

In this context, project visibility, the preferred term over project politics refers to the level of exposure and attention a particular project receives. This can be attributed to the individual's cognitive map or the priority given through the frequency of the projects being discussed, monitored, and tracked; be it at team, management or board level.

The existence of project visibility is widely accepted by various project management practitioners but least discussed out in the open. Differences in originating culture may be the cause, resulting in differing levels of acceptance and sensitivities. The outcome of my discussions with all the project owners confirms this reality.

Project visibility has a significant influence over both the level of top management support and project outcome. Considering this significant influence, *project visibility is the key success factor* that drives both top *management support* and in ensuring *project success.*

TRAPPED IN BETWEEN:
Realities of the project world

Battle of the "Biz Whiz": The boardroom and the project room

Ensuring project success is an uphill battle. It is such a tiring and painful journey that many have taken a fall. The war against project failures has many battles, and most of these battles were fought within the confined space of the company itself. Between the boardroom and the project room!

I have heard project consultants and practitioners preaching on the importance of certain projects to a company. Likewise, the importance of managing the critical success factors in order to achieve successful project closures is repeatedly drummed across. I have also observed many times, new terms and jargons being used in project proposals or project briefings at board, senior management as well as the working levels. Despite the explanation, clarification, amplification, and recommendations made by these experts, companies are *still stuck* with only small percentages of project success. A huge number of projects suffer from project derailments, suspensions or worst, die a natural death!

It is absurd that companies pay out professional fees to these experts, while they (the companies) themselves were performing "*the circus of project failures*". While the people within these companies were distressed and feeling sorry for themselves, these experts are smiling all the way to the bank. Food for thought: but how many companies chew on this?

In describing these real life situations, I will use scenarios and metaphors in order to maintain confidentiality of names and companies. Let it be known that, I too have to sign Non-Disclosure Agreements (NDAs) whenever I am assigned to major projects. However, I assure you that the integrity of the project contents and cases remains intact.

Let the battle begin!

THE AFX EMPIRE

AFX is a fictitious name given to illustrate a multimillion-dollar global Malaysian company and in my opinion is representative of other major conglomerates that I have closely associated.

My main reason for describing the brief history of AFX is to paint an overall mental image of the company to you. This is important for our discussions, as we should be viewing the same battlefield.

My reason for choosing the three-letter acronym is simple - AF is my initials and I simply like the alphabet X.

Since inception in 1971, AFX went through numerous management changes to ensure that the company remained as a viable entity.

AFX is a public listed company. A Chairman heads the Board of Directors, which is responsible for the formulation of the company's policies. A Managing Director (MD) heads the company's management team and is responsible for the daily operations as well as the wellbeing of the company. AFX received its first Chairman and first MD after the approval from the Government.

In the early years, AFX had focused its strategy and tactical decisions towards business operations. A 'black spot' in AFX history occurred when there was a disruption of services due to an industrial unrest from January to March 1979. The Government's intervention has helped to diffuse the situation and operations were back to normal in April 1979.

Following the incident, programs were introduced to rally staff support for the company's future growth. Various employee-relations' activities were carried out with high visibility of the management team. This had resulted in increased support from various levels of staff and management for the betterment of AFX.

In 1982, a second MD took over to head the management team. During his tenure, AFX went public and floated its share in 1985. This was the beginning of a new era; AFX acquired a new dimension and propelled itself as a business entity. Pressured by the global competition and changes in the geo-political and socio-economic environment, change programs were designed and implemented accordingly.

In 1986, in line with the Government's Look-East policy, AFX was instrumental in articulating the implementation of small work group activities known as Quality Control Circles ("**QCC**") within the company and at the national level. The Organisation Development Department (ODD) parked under Human Resource Division headed the program. The program was considered successful at operational level as many benefits, both qualitative and quantitative, were gained from such move.

As the application of QCC was gaining maturity, it was discovered that, for successful application across the company, the concept of quality management had to be applied at management level as well.

Hence, in 1989, the Company-Wide Quality Control ("**CWQC**") was developed and introduced. However, such introduction was rather short-lived. Although such a concept was very much understood at staff level, it did not get through to the management level. This was due to the working level staff having at least a four-year head start ahead of the managerial group. This resulted in a decline in the number of QCC activities across the company.

A UK based external consultant was engaged to conduct a research relating to the concerns of QCC and CWQC implementation, which led to the following discoveries:

- The program lacked the foundation layer such as 5s to sustain the momentum of QCC activities.
- To a certain degree, upward movement was hindered by the lack of management understanding on such initiatives.

- The initial implementation was rather a direct replicate from the Japanese concept; it did not take into consideration the socio-cultural differences existing within the company's workforce and its working organisation.
- Despite the decline in the number of QCC activities, it was not considered a total failure. This was because benefits reaped from the various initiatives could be felt across the company.

The whole programme was later reviewed incorporating the research findings. In 1991, "**DSE**" program was introduced headed by the same team (ODD). This program incorporated the foundation layer such as '5s', as well as cross-functional quality improvement teams (QIT) activities.

The whole intent of this program was to provide focus for all levels of staff, inclusive of the management team, towards achieving service excellence culture. In avoiding the same pitfall during the CWQC implementation, the management team were the first to be involved in the design and development of the program.

In 1992, a second Chairman was appointed to the board with the third MD heading the company's management team. Continuing the success, A DSE council was formed and personally chaired by the Managing Director himself. He made DSE progress status as part of the management meeting agenda. Training workshops, seminars, and road shows were conducted across all levels in the organisation to create awareness and buy-in from the population. Consequently, the number of improvement projects continued to grow.

It can be generally summarised that, in DSE, management drove the quality policies and staff drove the quality improvements. It was a 'win-win' situation for AFX's entire stakeholders where motivation and morale were at their peak.

A major swing took place in 1994, when a disposed subsidiary of AFX took majority control over the company's shareholdings. Upon the approval by the relevant authorities, the third Chairman became the company's Executive Chairman with a fourth MD appointed. Such a move was supposedly to further elevate AFX's standing in line with national aspirations. What was dubbed the **"TRANSFORMATION"** program replaced the DSE program.

The TRANSFORMATION program was carried out in *two phases*. The first phase, called **"TRANSFORMATION 1"** (T1) was launched in July 1997. It was developed to address the specific areas of business and operations with a timeframe of less than one year.

T1 was developed by some of the ODD team members in collaboration with a US based consulting group. The main activities for T1 were Creating Management Alignment, quick-hits initiatives on Customer Focus, Branding, Human Resources, Technology, and Communications.

The whole intent was to create *management alignment* and generate success stories through quick-hits initiatives to further enhance employees' buy-in. T1 was considered to be successful with some initiatives being carried across to the second phase known as **"TRANSFORMATION 2"** (T2). A full closure report was done prior crossing over into T2.

T2 headed by a fresh set of team members, was launched in May 1998. The scope of T2 was expanded to cover the total business operations of AFX. The timeframe suggested was over a period of three to five years. A new business model was introduced in line with the strategic alignment done in T1. T2 entailed the rationalisation of Customer Value Chain, Technical/Operational Support Chain, Subsidiaries Operations, and Business Support Services.

Due to the massive scope of the program, it was observed that the management of T2 was far from desired. There seemed to be a lack of focus on business direction, and the ability to close out improvement projects appeared weak.

Other organisational influences had also created tremendous pressure on T2. The Economic Crisis and rigorous preparations for the Year 2000 (Y2K) contingencies pushed the whole T2 program off track. The Asian Financial Crisis had further plunged AFX into deep losses.

The focus of T2 was perceived to be fuzzy and program leadership was greatly lacking due to the uncertainty of the Executive Chairman's position. In late 2000, both the Executive Chairman and Managing Director resigned. AFX was without proper figurehead. Consequently, the success of T2 was in doubt, as there was no evidence of a proper project closure being carried out.

The ailing AFX abolished the former Executive Chairman post and in 2001, upon approval by the relevant authorities, AFX appointed the fourth Chairman and the fifth MD to steer the company.

A "**TURNAROUND**" program was initiated replacing the ailing T2. The Managing Director himself, with assistance from a fresh team brought in from external consulting groups, headed the program.

In the initial stages, the TURNAROUND program content was seen to be all-encompassing, taking a holistic approach in the design and implementation. There were *three major streams* advocated: Financial, Communication, and Human Resources.

A sub-program that used a three-pronged approach (culture-resource-process) was introduced for the human resources stream. The intent is to prepare employees in meeting new challenges and supporting business goals and objectives.

However, over time, the overall effort was greatly focused towards *financial recovery*. Balance-sheet restructuring and cash flow management were the buzzwords. There were no apparent benefits gained from such move until the end of 2002, when the financial restructuring exercise was announced.

The financial restructuring exercise entailed the necessary transfers and sales of assets and liabilities to another entity, a special purpose vehicle (SPV) set up to straighten out the financial standing of AFX. This time, a local consulting firm was instrumental in the implementation.

As the focus was mainly on financials, other stakeholder expectations were seen as being compromised and resulted in low morale amongst the general population. I am not at the liberty to disclose occurrences and incidents that had occurred out of such frustrations and will refrain from making any further comments.

Upon expiry of this MD's term, in 2004, a sixth MD was appointed to head the company's management team. With the focus on winning customer confidence on the product and services provided by AFX, a program "**GBE**" was launched, attended by a huge crowd across all staff levels, a noble intent where all employees were expected to go the extra mile in exceeding the customer expectations.

Concerned with morale issues, AFX engaged an international research company that specialises in human resources survey to conduct a massive global employee survey.

While the program was in full swing, AFX received news on the sudden demise of the fourth Chairman. The staffs were deeply aggrieved and mourned for the loss at a time when AFX was moving aggressively towards recovery. Against the saddened atmosphere, the fifth Chairman was appointed in August 2004.

After holding the post for a year, the sixth MD stepped down in 2005 and the Chairman acted as both the Chairman and the Managing Director. While maintaining the fifth Chairman, the seventh MD was appointed to head another fresh management team in December 2005.

In February 2006, another program, "**BTP**" was unveiled. The pledge made during the launch was, BTP would not only reverse the loss and return AFX into profitability, but also transform AFX into a strong and vibrant institution capable of withstanding the external shocks and tracking new opportunities. Similar to the previous change program, the BTP builds upon five central thrust that is, Commercial, Operations, Finance, People, and Stakeholders.

This change of guards within AFX has created multiple impacts on the way change programs were developed, designed, and implemented.

I hope you are now able to form a mental image of AFX as we proceed with the battles.

BATTLE NO.1: TRANSFORMATION, MUTATION OR ASSIMILATION

AFX is never short of change programs and program names. Operationally, AFX has not recovered fully from ailments suffered since the financial crisis, despite the change programs brought about by the changes at helm.

The question frequently asked by the masses is, "How could this still happen?" In every change program communications, there were claims made that the previous change programs lack the critical ingredients to pull the company out of the red.

Well, I am no accountant, but in my opinion, financial results are a translation of how effective and efficient AFX are. If we are effective, that is, *doing the right things*, we should be generating enough revenue for the company. Likewise, if we are efficient, that is, *doing things right*, we should be able to contain a major part of our operating costs. Basing on such opinion, the changes introduced by AFX could be ineffective or inefficient, or both.

Numerous questions linger around most of the loyal subjects who have given their hearts and souls for AFX.

"What is actually wrong with AFX?"

"Is AFX addressing the real problems or merely treating the symptoms?"

"Was there sufficient time given for the teams (management and employees) to manoeuvre the programs and see it through before effecting the next change?"

"Was there really a transformation?"

"Has the fresh team introduced into AFX assimilated by the existing culture?"

"Has the induced culture mutated itself into something that is more change resistant?"

Attempts to answer the above questions not only put pressure on the board of directors, management team, and employees, but also placed tremendous pressure on the program directors, project managers, and team members.

Welcome to realities of the project world!

Scene No.1

During the January to April 1979 period, it could be seen that the employee relations program was specifically designed to diffuse the industrial unrest in AFX. Moderation by the Government (which took the role of program director) managed to place both parties (management and staff) at the same table. Participation by both the management team and staff created a balance of power and trust. Being the first ever major incident in the history of AFX, both parties were willing to settle the dispute in the spirit of goodwill and learning from each other's mistakes. An excellent approach indeed!

Of course, there were demands and expectations put forward by both parties. However, not all of the demands, needs, and expectations were met, and most of the agreements reached were done through compromises. Some like to term this "win-win", but in my opinion, reaching agreements through compromises is *not* meeting needs or expectations, as compromises led to many trade-offs.

Various employee-relations initiatives were introduced. As much as financial resources were needed to fund these initiatives, it was done within the technical competencies of AFX. You would agree with me that, in managing a program of this scale, the realities of being "politically correct" are now primary and right at the top of the list.

The choice of who becomes the project manager or even the activities to be undertaken may not satisfy both parties, but was accepted basing on political understanding. This is the reality and it is something that beyond meeting the customer requirements or stakeholder expectations that I have mentioned in the *preface*.

Did things changed?

There were varied opinions from different quarters within AFX. Some are of the opinion that the actions and behaviours in reaching the agreements had surfaced the weaknesses within the management team of AFX, while the others are of the opinion that, such incident has elevated the culture of AFX to a new level.

Whichever the case may be, the culture within AFX has mutated into the next level and has transformed AFX into a new state, for better or for worse.

Scene No.2

The small workgroup activities known as Quality Control Circles (QCC) introduced in 1986 were mainly targeted at operational staff. Training workshops, communication seminars, and road shows were conducted on a regular basis. A program office under the Organisational Development Department (ODD) managed the whole program. Sufficient budget was allocated for the program commensurate with the growth in the number of circles. Within specified boundaries, the circles were free to introduce and implement improvement projects. They were allowed to participate in the national and regional level competitions. Successful that they were, they bagged numerous awards and accolades for their achievements and for the company. These workgroups' contributions have benefited AFX operationally and strategically. AFX had managed to champion the QCC activities nationwide as well as at regional levels resulting in a positive image and branding for AFX.

The challenge for the program manager back then was to balance the interplay between technical, financial and political viability of the program.

Convincing the board and the management team on both the technical and financial viability of the program was a tough battle. Since QCC was done within small workgroups, the financial returns brought about by these teams were minimal when compared with the total investment.

However, since the program was in-line with the government's Look-East policy, and had created more intangible benefits to AFX; the board and management team were willing to fund the program. There was huge political mileage to be gained by all parties involved in the program. Such covert agenda may be camouflaged by the rhetoric: "winning the support and gaining the trust of the employees is beyond any financial computations" filled the air, under the spirit of goodwill and trust.

So, was there really a change occurring within AFX?

Again, there were varied opinions on this. The winning program did change AFX into a new state, championing the QCC activities at both national and regional level. There were both tangible and intangible benefits gained from the program. The tangible results were in the form of savings, process improvements, and enhancements to service deliveries. As for the intangible benefits, the program made everyone in AFX "look good". Everyone was proud to be part of AFX. Cashing in on the political mileage and masking the hidden agenda through rhetoric speeches existed in any battles be they at the level of projects, programs, or organisations. Hence, a vast majority are of the opinion that this is an accepted norm for "*assimilation of the masses*" into a new way of life.

Scene No.3

After running the QCC program for about four years (1986-1989) and despite its great success, the program office (ODD) now faced a bigger challenge. The initial excitement of QCC was beginning to fade!

Since QCC was targeted more for the lower ranking staff, almost three-quarters of team members came from the operational (production) areas. Being in the production lines, they work a three-shift pattern. As in any production lines, staffs working on shifts get moved around according to production demands. Although the project leaders (circle leaders) had made requests for all the members to be working on the same shift, more often than not such requests were turned down due to the operational requirements. This had put a strain on the circles' activities.

As part of the company's contribution and support to the program, the project teams (circle members) were given an hour per week in the form of time-off for them to conduct the circle activities.

As an alternative solution to shift problems, affected staffs were requested to use their off-days to attend circle activities and later claim back the one-hour from the shift work. Some teams attempted to adopt such proposal but found it difficult when it came to their claims. Over time, these claims accumulated, as time-off requests were turned down due to the operational requirements. These backlogs of claims that constituted as staff privileges are now becoming an issue.

This issue was escalated to the program manager. Discussions between production supervisors, executives, and project leaders were scheduled in the presence of the production head. The intent of such meeting was to facilitate solution finding, and all parties were given the opportunity to air their views and opinions.

There were exchange of opinions, justification, and rationalisation between the parties involved. Despite the elaboration and presentations made by the program manager and the project leaders, the production executives insisted that the main reason for rejecting these claims were due to operational requirements. An ammunition that is hard to counter!

The episode finally ended with a clanger when the production head posed a question, *"which is more important, coming to work and doing time on the production line or getting involved in all these time wasting activities?"*

The program manager was stunned with such a question while the project leaders remained calm, as they have been asked the same question before.

"That is why we need you, the program manager, to come in and sort this matter out for us" said one of the project leaders to the program manager. *"We intend to bring this issue to our union's attention, as the company did not keep their part of the bargain"* while pausing for response.

Feeling threatened, the production head stood up and yelled, *"you can bring the mother of all the unions and I am not afraid to face them!"*

His face was flaming red and adrenalin running high as he continued, *"Operational requirement is management prerogative and I have the right to decide!"* slamming the door loudly as he left the room.

The program manager caught in a trap!
Trapped between the battle of the boardroom and the project room.

It is a known fact that the management team (the board inclusive) supported the program and were willing to give due recognition for such activities, and staffs were willing to participate enthusiastically.

So, what happened to the change and the assimilation?

Let us take a journey into the past by turning back the clock slightly. In late 1987, there was a minor change to the structure within AFX and as usual, few heads had to be moved around. One of the production senior executives was promoted to become the new production head.

This new production head was seen as an unpredictable and temperamental person, whose interest is purely in getting the production line into full swing; and been nicknamed "slave-driver" by the production staffs. He is good performer with clean records of accomplishment, and had good relationship with the bosses. Under his supervision, the production line was almost at 90% productivity with an excellent turnaround time performance. He was indeed the kind _any_ management would love to have, and in this case, an excellent candidate for promotion. However, he despised any activity that in his opinion was unrelated to the job being paid. He believed that staffs are paid to do time on the production line and nothing else.

That was how; the initial excitement of QCC activities begins to fades. Circle members were complaining about their production executives or supervisors for not giving them enough support.

Such issues, if brought to the union's attention can result in undesirable consequences for the program.

If we think that there were insufficient buy-in from management and staff, there were enough being done since 1986. Given that project leaders in other business areas were not affected, this issue is not a company-wide problem and can be considered an isolated case. However, no matter how isolated the case may be, this issue was affecting almost three quarter of the project team members' population within AFX.

A number to be reckoned with!

In getting out of the trap, the program manager had to tread very carefully without jeopardising the balance between the program needs against production needs. Again, the realities of the project world have surfaced!

Technically, all the projects were viable and all parties were right, depending on the each other's perspective. The management team were willing to grant privileges for staff activities, the staffs were willing to participate enthusiastically and the production head is indeed the suitable candidate for the position, give and take some attitudinal adjustment. Suffice to say, in cases like this, the program manager had to revert to the political realities in getting the production head be assimilated with the rest of the masses, and align his belief and stand on employee participation in change program.

Meaning, the program manager needed to politically strategies and get the buy-in of the production head.

Scene No.4

Since 1997, AFX went through numerous changes brought about by the different Managing Directors. The changes also included the placement of fresh management team members and other influential personnel within the system. As usual, there will be both major and minor restructuring exercises with new faces taking over the business areas as well as project ownership and sponsorship. Despite these changes, AFX still suffered huge losses operationally.

Was there really a transformation? Or was it simply mutation and assimilation?

It was noted that most of the change programs within AFX started with a right footing, by taking the *holistic* view of change. Both the human and non-human issues were considered and incorporated into the program design. Unfortunately, as the implementation progressed, the focus went astray. Too much emphasis placed on non-human issues such as financial results have compromised the human resources initiatives. Recruitment, training and development, promotions and succession plans became casualties of budget war.

In any change program launching, the keynote address would state, *"people are the most important assets the company have"*. The question posed by many of the loyal subjects, still remain unanswered is *"Which people, the existing ones or the new ones? "* This is a strong message especially if comes from the majority of employees.

Since the financial restructuring in 2002, the only assets left with AFX are their human resources. In my observations, it is *this* group of asset that is most frequently compromised and neglected in any change initiatives.

Concerned with the low productivity and morale within AFX, a global employee survey was conducted in early 2005. Results of the human resources survey conducted by AFX revealed the following:

- The surveys indicated a unique result of high Employee Engagement Index (EEI) amongst the employees. Employee's engagement scored the highest and was significantly way ahead of both the national norms and Global High Performance Companies. It reflected a *tremendous pride and respect for the company's reputation and brand.*
- Amongst the fifteen (15) variables established, *leadership scored the lowest* and significantly lagged (way too far) behind both the national norms and Global High Performance Companies.
- Weak scores in most other areas suggested a *collective negative perception towards the overall employee experience* in the company. The findings also reflected a seeming *gap between management and employee relationship.*
- The *culture* of being secretive, short-term oriented, directive but indecisive *does not complement* AFX global ambitions.

In my opinion, the results of such employee survey clearly indicated that AFX had not been addressing the <u>*real*</u> issue since 1997. The long neglected issue has now surfaced itself in an alarming manner.

This goes back to the question that I have posted earlier. "Was there really a transformation, or is it simply mutation and assimilation of convenience?"

A question that will linger around for quite some time and only the people within AFX have the answer.

In any battle, such realities will haunt program and project managers if effective counter measures are not properly thought of and put in place.

BATTLE NO.2: THE "BRAVE-SOULS" DIE FIRST

The battle begins with a project consultant (expert) representing the solution providers, giving a project proposal briefing attended by some board members, the senior management team members and the supposedly the project team members. While the briefing is taking place, the following scenes were observed.

Scene No.1: The lack of understanding on program and project management on my part, does not allow me to completely comprehend the subject being discussed; but I was too shy to ask, as it would make me look like a fool! That is the last thing that I want to happen. Being invited to attend the proposal's briefing means that I must be an important person, so I think! Avoiding any embarrassment, I would rather stay quiet and pretend as if I understand the subject perfectly well. The briefing adjourns and everyone leaves.

At the earliest available opportunity, I now begin quoting and using those terms mentioned by the experts at senior management meetings, departmental meetings and even at staff briefings. This will prove to the masses that I am project management savvy and I belong to the same team. Even if I don't have a clue as to what the terms *actually* mean!

I could sense that some of you readers are giving me that cynical smile. You may have observed similar phenomena within your organisation, or you yourself have been there. In either case, you have now stepped into the realm of wisdom!

Scene No.2: The lack of understanding on program and project management on the presenters' end (so called experts) has created a total confusion amongst the listeners, but again the listeners were too shy to ask; as it would make the listeners look like fools! That is the last thing that anybody wants to happen. Being invited to attend the proposal's briefing shows that they (the listeners) are important individuals. Likewise, to avoid any embarrassment, the listeners would rather stay quiet and pretend as if they understand the subject perfectly well. Again, the briefing adjourns and everyone leaves.

Similar to scene No.1, at the earliest available opportunity, these individuals will begin quoting and using the terms used by the presenters (so-called experts) at senior management meetings, departmental meetings and even at staff briefings. This will prove to the masses that they (the listeners) are project management savvy and belong to the same team, even if they don't have a clue as to what the terms *actually* mean!

Scene No.3: I like this part and just love building on this scenario. The lack of understanding on program and project management on the presenters' end (so-called experts) has created a total confusion amongst the listeners, but this time is slightly different. Somebody within the crowd who is well informed and a learned person, whom I call the "*brave-soul*" was not shy to ask; even if it will make the him or her look like a fool! That is the last thing any presenter wants to happen, unless he or she is very clear about the subject. Which in this case, he or she is NOT!

Being flown in from hundreds or maybe thousands of miles to conduct the presentation, the presenter must be an important person. He or she must be the CEO or A Senior Partner or at the very least the Marketing Director of the firm. To avoid any embarrassment, the presenter will begin citing his or her involvement in previous projects costing million of dollars, carried out in some major blue chip companies, in some famous global cities.

Now comes the interesting part. Although in complete control of the situation, (well, that is what they are trained for!) the presenter begins to fumble. Half of the citations may be facts, while the remaining half sounds more like "garnishing the menu", using some arbitrary cases with the tendency of using bigger, and wilder jargon, resulting in more confusion! Other participants refuse to indulge, as they (other participants) do not wish to be branded as "incapable of comprehending" the subject being discussed.

What will happen next is, the *"brave-soul"* will be requested to remain quiet and not prolong the session. Such request would come from higher-ranking officials, as they are having an afternoon working lunch cum golf session to attend. The presenter feels that the issues were excellently addressed, though in reality, they were not. Satisfied with the presentation, the briefing adjourns and everyone leaves.

There were varied opinions formed by the participants on this particular scene.

Being influential, the presenter managed to convince the management team to exclude the *"brave-soul"* from the project team. "This is a typical example of those who resist change and are stuck with the old regime ideologies", they say.

Of course, some would be in agreement with the presenter. In any change, there are bound to be forces that work for and against; and "maybe this is the one that works against", some said. If the *"brave-soul"* is as good as he or she claim to be, then "AFX would not be in the situation that they are in right now, still facing difficulties to get out from the losses", they conclude.

Suffice to say that the *"brave-soul"* was dropped from the project team list, never to be heard of again.

However, there were those in agreement with the *"brave-soul"* but would rather keep their opinions to themselves. After seeing so many change programs that profess the same things, over-and-over again, this *"brave-soul"* is right! These new faces don't understand what the *"brave-soul"* is trying to say, they whisper silently.

I don't have to detail out what happen to the *"brave-soul"*, as your guesses are as good as mine. Nevertheless, the point that I am putting across is that, the *"brave-soul"* die first!

Inferences

From the above three scenes, there are a couple of inferences that can be learnt by program and project managers in addressing the realities.

Try to get as much information on the proposed project prior to attending the presentations. Through your circle of network, ask whether they have heard about the project. News on major projects requiring major funding with the involvement of senior management personnel travels like wild fire across the company. This will give you a fair idea of the importance of such project.

Try to find out more about the consulting firm or the company that is giving the presentations. Are they really as good as they claim to be? Internet search can be a good place to start. Please don't get me wrong. There are excellent consulting firms such as BCG, KPMG, Gartner and Standish, to cite a few, specific to industries and businesses. I have personally met some of these excellent consultants on change, program and project management and IT solutions and their works are being quoted in journals, magazines, and books.

You would sense that something is not right, if for example, an external auditing firm that went bust due to poor corporate governance were to present to you on how excellent their corporate governance model for you to adopt. Right?

Even if your *common sense* tells you that something is not right, try to find out more on how this firm gained entry into your system. Was it part of an open tender or bidding exercise or is somebody influential within your organisation bringing them in? This will give you a fair idea on who is in favour or supporting the firm's presence.

Upon gathering the necessary information, try to ask the organiser, who else were invited and make great effort to attend the presentation. If somebody influential is behind the firm, you will see an array of senior officials and management team making their way into the presentation room. The project and the firm giving the presentation are important and supported respectively.

If you find out that no senior officials and or management team members are attending, and most of the participants are from the middle or junior level executives, then the support of such a firm is in doubt, even if the project is important.

This is your *reality* check, the realities of project politics!

By having more information in advance, you are able to position yourself accordingly during the session, unless you want to be one of the *"brave-souls"* who die first!

I have read somewhere claiming that there is a difference between the Western and the Eastern culture on this sort of behaviours. There were claims made that the Western project culture is more liberal, open to debate, and confrontational with no personal vendetta; while the Eastern project culture is the reverse. Unfortunately, basing on my project experiences in both cultures, this did not seem so! In my opinion, the project culture was observed to be *similar* when it boils down to above three scenes and inferences.

The moral of the story gathered from this battle is, *"brave-souls"* will die first while the *"wise-ones"* survive hoping to claim the victory and the glory, if they are not annihilated.

BATTLE NO.3: ANNIHILATION OF THE "WISE-ONE"

Inferring from Battle No.2, we could see that there exist those who are in agreement with the "*brave-soul*" but remain silent. They have either served the company long enough to understand the politics of change program and projects, or they have once been a wounded "*brave-soul*".

Looking at the history of AFX, changes at the helm and the management team have taken place almost once every *three years* since 1997. In every change program introduced, *new faces from differing industries* were placed to steer the company, the change program and projects.

The purpose of such a move is to rejuvenate AFX with presumably high-calibre "*fresh blood*" to counter the deadly virus created by the mutated culture as described in Battle No.1. A noble intent, I must say.

However, despite these efforts, AFX still has not recovered from its ailments and is still suffering from operational losses.

What is wrong with AFX?

In attempting to answer the question, the formed opinion is based on the events and discussions that I had, and I will describe the events using metaphors and scenarios. Hopefully this can be a *lesson learnt* for all of us, whenever we are recruited into a new company or a new workplace.

In my opinion, these "*fresh blood*" were indeed high-calibre and vibrant. Most of them were brought in from the same consulting firm, which was preferred by the newly appointed MD in 2001. Unfortunately, they were genetically modified prior their induction into AFX. As such, these "*fresh blood*" contain *genetic impurities*.

I had the opportunity to discuss with these "*fresh blood*" during their induction phases into AFX where I asked a few simple and basic questions.

   "What were the challenges that you have accepted to be in?"

"What was the picture painted to you on AFX and its people before you were brought in?"

"What was your formed perception or opinion concerning AFX?"

My intent was to establish, if there existed any preconceived opinion or prejudgement made prior to induction with AFX. I call this process as *seeking genetic impurities*. Basing on my experience, this is crucial for any change program and project design and implementations. Denying this fact will mean that we are denying the realities of the project world.

The following represents some of the extracts during my discussions with these "*fresh blood*".

The challenge put forward as claimed by them was, "we are given the task to turnaround AFX as we could not rely on the existing people to do it".

They claimed that even the MD was saying, "There are not enough good people to manoeuvre the change and I need people that I am confident and comfortable with, as I myself am a stranger in AFX."

I noted their response and continued further by asking, "Are you familiar with the core business of AFX?" The purpose is to establish their level of familiarity concerning the business that they were about to get themselves involved in.

Their responses were, "Although the core business of AFX is unique, we reckon that it will be the same with other businesses and turnaround programs".

"What do you mean by that?" I interjected.

"Since it involves major financial restructuring and we have done it before, we believe we can do it here," they said.

When I sensed some resentment on their part, I faded the discussions by welcoming them to the team.

Later in the month, I accidentally met one of the human resources (HR) staff and asked him how these *"fresh blood"* got into the system. He said, "They were hand picked by the MD".

I further asked the HR staff, "What are their backgrounds?"

Without going into specifics, suffice to say that the majority of them were accountants with auditing and financial background, and with about five years working experience. I was not surprised, as the majority of them were fresh recruits of an external auditing firm before it wound up.

"Is there anybody with human resources background, majoring in Industrial Relation or Organisation Development?" I asked.

"Nope, I wish there are, as we need one here badly!" the HR staff quickly replied.

Whenever a new MD takes the post, there is a tendency of bringing a fresh team that they are comfortable to work with. I guess such behaviours are common and acceptable practice anywhere. I don't think there is anything wrong in that!

However, what goes on behind the scenes does matter; and may be detrimental to the project outcomes for the change program in AFX.

I consider it as normal for all these newly appointed MDs to be given a tall order to turn around AFX. However, publicising their appointments in both the local and foreign media and splashing their prior achievements have increased stakeholders' hopes and expectations for speedy recovery. This puts unnecessary pressure on every newly appointed MD and I don't envy them one bit!

However, basing on my earlier discussions with the *"fresh blood"* it seems like these newly appointed MDs lack the trust and confidence in the existing management team and employees at large. How could anyone blame him? After all, AFX is still struggling to recover from huge operational losses.

Nevertheless, secretly passed remarks amongst these *"fresh blood"* indicate that, the MD has a preconceived opinion and has prejudged AFX and its employees even before stepping in. The genetic impurities have <u>no</u> mercy; even the MD is not immune!

This will make him, consciously or unconsciously, to shut every door for any ideas or opinions from the existing team within AFX; the team that he is supposedly leading.

In any battle of opinions, the following outcome can happen caused by these genetic impurities. Number one, being externally recruited from differing industry, the MD's defence shield will be fully charged whenever he senses inadequacy within him.

"Inadequacy? How could this be so?" you might ask.

Well, how could it not be so, when three-quarters of the discussion's contents centred on the business that he is not familiar with! This will lead to number two; where out of his ignorance, arrogance comes into effect. His missile tubes will be fully 'charged-up' and ready to launch against existing management team and employees of AFX as vulnerable targets. Questions like "If you are so good, why is it AFX is in such a critical state?" Such question will shut everyone up! Don't you think so?

In either outcome, this is not a good sign!

For those *"fresh blood"* who receives unconditional support from the MD will now start working their way into the system. They will be dismantling and reconstructing new business models at every corner of the businesses including areas that they are not familiar with.

Sharing with you a case, these *"fresh blood"* demolished all the previously created project offices and reconstructed a newly formed Project Management Department (PMD), managed and staffed by new recruits, meaning more *"fresh blood"*. In my opinion, setting up a central PMD overseeing all the projects within AFX is indeed a superb idea. Unfortunately, since the majority of these *"fresh blood"* were consultants with either accounting or auditing qualifications, none of them was actually having <u>real</u> project management experience or qualifications. Project management knowledge was acquired as part of their studies during college days and qualifications such as Project Management Professional (PMP®) was never heard off. Since the fate of the PMD was entrusted to these *"fresh blood"*, my guess is that, PMD set up will not last long.

When I asked the existing population, "why don't they advise and guide these *"fresh blood"*?

Their cynical response was, "Well, we thought they knew what they were doing as they were the high-calibre *"fresh blood"* handpicked by the MD", (and continues) "after all, they don't want to listen to us as they said that they have done it before!"

Another bad sign, I say to myself.

The outcome of my discussions and observations clearly indicate that there is a bad omen occurring and history shall repeat itself.

Finally, my premonition comes true!

True enough; unclear with the whole intent and purpose of setting up the PMD, the Department was shut down two years later. These *"fresh blood"* were redeployed to other business areas continuing their trail of destruction.

My observations shows that, these genetically modified *"fresh blood"*, contains genetic impurities, and are contaminated with a virus-causing syndrome; a syndrome that I called, *Deceived by Own Perception* (DOPer).

According to a medical encyclopaedia that I read elsewhere, syndrome is defined as "a group of symptoms and or signs occurring together, constituting a particular disorder".

The particular disorder caused by these contaminated blood was most prominent in the host's behaviour and mindset. It forms a false perception within the host's mind that makes the host to *believe that they completely know what they actually don't know*. The symptoms and or signs occurring together would be what we normally termed as *ignorance, arrogance,* and *egotism* amongst others.

Hence, people suffering from "DOPer" Syndrome are considered as "a group or individuals that are oblivious to what they don't know, and yet behaving as if they are completely in the know"; mind-boggling isn't it?

Metaphorically, it is like a bachelor (unmarried man or woman) who has never lost any of his or her family members trying to comfort someone who has just lost his or her child in a bad car accident, by saying *"I know what you are going through"*. I know we should feel sorry for the loss but sometimes; we ought to be realistic when it comes to empathy, especially when we haven't been there before.

Likewise, in change programs and projects. I have observed individuals sometimes consciously or unconsciously deceiving themselves with things that they themselves are not familiar with.

Program and project managers must be fully aware and alert that "DOPer" Syndrome has no mercy; anyone can be infected! Since "DOPer" is all about perception and mindset, denying this syndrome is a recipe for disaster!

Anyway, out of such syndrome exhibited by these *"fresh blood"*, gradually, all those caring employees, with vast knowledge and experiences, were disassociated from the initiatives within the program and projects; and leaving the MD and his *"fresh-blood"* to turnaround AFX.

Hence, the annihilation of the "wise-one" has begun!

BATTLE NO.4: THE IRREVERSIBLE FALL

There are two things that I enjoy doing, photography and cooking. In photography, I like capturing the moods and expressions of the subjects; while in cooking, I like trying out new recipes.

Whenever I am trying out a new recipe, I am very cautious with what I put inside the concoction that I am brewing. I have to admit that not all of my attempts were successful. For unsuccessful attempts, there are three options made available to me.

The *first* option is to completely throw out the concoction and start fresh. It sounds bad throwing out food while there are people suffering from malnutrition and insufficient food supply out there. However, trying to correct a "foul dish" may result in it getting worse, I may end up spending more time, effort, and other resources trying to get it right, which does not make any sense!

The *second* option is for me to request the assistance from another cook or a chef to do the necessary correction or tweak the concoction. Being a chef, he or she will be asking me what sort of a dish I want to create and what I have done before this. That will give him or her fair idea about the dish that I intend to create.

The *third* option is for me to request someone else who is oblivious to cooking to do the necessary corrections. Without trying to understand what has been done before, the person will then attempt to correct the concoction basing on his or her opinion on what the dish is supposed to taste and look like. In this instance, two possibilities may arise. One, the dish may turn out well and the other, the dish will get worse. In either case, the concoction is subjected to the *elements of chance*.

In looking at AFX from the similar perspective, I will use the 'classic' case of Performance Management System (PMS) project and illustrate to you how changes in AFX have affected the project. There are two reasons why I call this PMS project a 'classic'. *One*, the PMS project is a typical representation of other major multi-million dollar projects that turned sour; and *two*, PMS never get to live long enough in AFX even until the year 2006.

AFX has a rich history of change. If you notice, changes within AFX had been occurring at a more rapid pace past the year 1992. In case you have missed it, don't worry, I will re-enlighten you on the changes while making the necessary linkages to the PMS project.

Please allow me to describe to you some of the incidents that happened during the period 1992-2006, for you to draw your own opinion.

Before 1992, following the industrial unrest, AFX introduced a PMS project for employees in the executive grades and above. It was called "**PAR**". PAR adopted a concept similar to that of management by objectives (MBO). However, still governed by the associations' collective agreements, PAR served merely as a tool in staff's succession planning and development exercises. There was no direct link to the reward system and everyone was being paid basing on the agreed pay structure.

In 1992, AFX promoted an *internal* senior official as a third MD with the same management team. A change program known as DSE was introduced. Within the program, an enhanced PMS project called "**PRIDE**" was introduced for the employees in the managerial grades.

PRIDE incorporated more enhancements as compared with the previous PAR system. Although the DSE program was considered by many as successful in totality, PRIDE was still not linked to the reward system and everyone was being paid basing on the agreed pay structure, governed by the unions and associations' collective agreements.

Circa 1984-1994, PAR was allowed to grow into PRIDE. Both PAR and PRIDE was developed using internal talents in consultation with other successful organisations. The main driver for PRIDE was the DSE program that was seen as successful by the general population. There were sufficient lobbying with the unions and the associations that govern the salary structure through the respective collective agreements. Even some of the unions and associations executive committee members formed part of the training resources. While the acceptance of PRIDE by the target groups was excellent, AFX was slow in linking PRIDE to the reward system.

PRIDE was technically and financially a viable project. However, failure to capitalise on the available opportunities had made PRIDE, a project that is not politically correct to certain groups within AFX. Perceptions of '*employees were being intimidated*' by the company and the '*subtle loss of power and influence*' by the unions and associations grew stronger as PRIDE outcomes were slow and not forthcoming.

When the program and project managers were negotiating with the board, the unions, and the associations, changes at the helm took place. PRIDE was never given a chance to grow further but suffered *infant mortality* when another PMS project was introduced.

In 1994, two *external* figures were appointed as the third Chairman/Executive Chairman and the fourth MD respectively. An entirely new program known as TRANSFORMATION replaced the DSE program and concurrently, minor changes to the management team were made. With these changes, DSE and PRIDE were terminated.

Unhappy with the lack of a formal performance management system, the management team launched a new PMS project known "**PEP**", again to the same group, that is, employees in the managerial grades. Not taking a lesson from the past PMS projects, a fresh set of consultants and team members were brought in to manage the project.

I was fortunate enough to discuss the project with the fresh group (**FG**) and manage to ask them some fundamental questions. Like always, described below are some of my discussions extracts.

AF: "looks like PEP is similar to the previous PAR and PRIDE projects. Have you checked with the previous team on what actually happened?"

FG: "Shooooshhhh!" (immediate response requesting me to keep my tone down)

AF: (such response surprised me and on reflex), "What did I say wrong?"

FG: (In a slow tone) "Please refrain from mentioning PRIDE or DSE or anything that was done by the previous management"

AF: "Why?" (I hastily asked in a similar tone).

FG: "People up there (the new management) do not like to hear anything about what the previous management did. It is considered taboo!"

The room was dead silent with twenty-four eyeballs focus-locked on me. It was like everyone turned zombies and I could even hear a pin dropped!

AF: "Could anyone here be kind enough to explain to me what exactly I have missed?" (I asked the fresh team calmly).

After a comprehensive explanation, I discovered that, the new management team had had a bad encounter with the human resources department. "*Seems like all the employee records were in a mess*", the fresh group said.

AF: "That's not new, please tell me something new!"

FG: "Seems like the management team was looking for any potential individuals that could be identified to head certain business areas. To their nightmare, they lived to find out that there is nothing of such effect in the staff files. It's just like the X-files you know.., The truth is out there, somewhere".

The management team was furious and asked, "What happened to those PRIDE and DSE programs that you guys bragged about so much?"

One of the new management team members further said, "You guys are a bunch of idiots that doesn't know what you are doing! No wonder you are in such a mess! I am bringing in a new project team do it and may be you guys can learn from them." The fresh project team ended the so-called debriefing.

Remember what I wrote about project politics earlier? Now comes the interesting part.

During the period 1994-2000, a change in the management team took place. Oblivious to the issues and challenges of the previous PRIDE project, a fresh external team was brought in to implement the PEP project. Even though the project ran for two years, some of the project stakeholders, namely the managerial group, unions and associations had lost their confidence in the PEP project.

PEP was perceived as a 'form filling' exercise and was experiencing a low submission rate especially towards the tail end of the project. Regardless of the managers' achievements and their submission status, no one was either rewarded or reprimanded, as PEP was still not linked to the reward and recognition system.

Like PRIDE, PEP was technically and financially a viable project. However, failure to comprehend and address the challenges brought about by PRIDE implementation had made PEP a victim of circumstances. Battles between the board, project team, unions and associations had made PEP a project that was not *politically correct* in AFX.

Again, the program and project managers were caught in a trap; A trap with no way out!

As news concerning the departure of the Executive Chairman and the MD grew stronger, interest in PEP project quickly diminished. In late 2000, the PMS project, PEP, died a *natural death* for the second time!

In early 2001, an *external* figure was appointed as the fifth MD to steer AFX. TURNAROUND program replaced the ailing TRANSFORMATION program. The Managing Director recruited a fresh team from external consulting groups to form part of the new management team. Operationally, AFX still suffered from losses but through a financial restructuring exercise, AFX manage to show better results.

Another entirely new PMS project labelled as **"PMS-KPI"** was introduced for the same group. Since PMS-KPI adopted the Balanced Scorecard (BSC) approach, a new set of consultants, RF Consulting (a fictitious name), was engaged to design and implement the project. There was a big project launch with the consultants conducting various workshops and road shows.

Suffice to say, the project ran for two years, which consisted of two-performance cycles. Like the previous PEP project, PMS-KPI was still not linked to the reward system.

In 2004, an *internal* senior executive was promoted as the sixth MD, with the management team remaining intact. A program called GBE was launched to restore customer and investor confidence. The new MD endorsed the continuation of PMS-KPI into the next cycle.

During the period 2000-2005, a number of interesting events that took place.

In 2002, with approval from the MD, a new HR Manager, MJ (a fictitious name) was recruited externally to work with RF Consulting and to head the PMS-KPI project. Contractually, the consultants worked with and guided the project team for six months, and left upon expiry of their contract.

Although unsupported, there were strong rumours that, the nine-month old newly recruited HR Manager, MJ, decided to resign; as he felt that the scope of the PMS-KPI project was way beyond his capability. A noble action I must say, holstering his side arm knowing he would loose the battle!

The Head of Human Resources (appointed circa 2000/2001) turned down MJ's resignation. Instead, MJ was counter offered a higher salary and a new portfolio. Of course, MJ accepted the offer and later withdrew his resignation letter. You and I would have done the same, wouldn't we? Not only was one extracted from the field before engaging the battle, but also given a medal of honour. It would be silly to reject!

Following this turn of events, the project was put on hold for about three months. Again, with approval from the MD, another new HR Manager, FH (a fictitious name) was recruited externally to take over the position vacated by MJ. The newly appointed manager, FH, took over as the PMS-KPI project manager, leading the same project team.

As one of the user-group project director, I was keen to profile the PMS-KPI project for my own research especially after learning about the recent episodes. Described below are some of my discussions extracts with FH.

AF: "Looks like PMS-KPI is similar to the Balanced Scorecard (BSC) approach, have you checked with the project team as to what actually happened previously?"

FH: "I was made to understand that there were too much resistance from the managers."

AF: "Wow, this is news to me! Tell me more, if you don't mind".

FH: "The consultants did not do a good job as most of the managers were still not clear on the whole PMS-KPI processes".

I was beginning to like her until she uttered the following statement:

FH: "We need to engage a consultant, who specialises in BSC implementation to help us."

AF: "Gossh!!! Weren't the previous consultants specialist in BSC, and you, being a PMS expert?"

FH: "Well, I don't consider myself as an expert, but I was in charge of PMS implementation in my previous firm. Also, I don't have the opportunity to totally review what the previous manager did, but that was how it was explained to me".

Out of courtesy, I briefly described to her the chain of events and later handed her my opinion. "Of course, that is my opinion, and I stand corrected", as I closed my history lesson. Although she thanked me, I could see her face turning blue as if she had seen a ghost!

I do not actually know what happened next, but six months later, there was some minor restructuring exercise within the Human Resources Department. FH was reassigned to perform other tasks. Again, the PMS-KPI project was left without a project manager. Within the next couple of weeks, there was an announcement made. An internal senior executive, RX (a fictitious name), who was working on this PMS project since 1992 was promoted to Manager and became the third PMS-KPI project manager.

Although it was an internal affair, such news travelled across the company like wild fire. All the employees in the managerial grade knew RX as they have been working closely with him since PRIDE days.

The question posed by these employees in the managerial grades was, "Why does AFX have to recruit two external managers, later to find out that both of them were incapable of performing the task, yet keep them and later promote someone from within to do the job?"

This question has remained unanswered.

As I have mentioned in battle No.3, those genetic impurities could have clouded the judgement of certain key individuals or groups within AFX.

Meanwhile, the PMS-KPI continued without any link to the reward system; and finally died a *natural death* for the third time.

After running PAR, PRIDE, PEP, and PMS-KPI for a number of cycles with different owners and project managers, the PMS projects' outcomes haven't got close to the existing reward system. Consequently, a majority the stakeholders who happened to be those in the managerial grades, lost their confidence in the system.

In late 2005, an external figure was appointed the seventh MD to head another fresh management team recruited externally. A "BTP" program was unveiled. Within the BTP, the performance management system (PMS) was promised to be more robust and future rewards will be closely linked to the Balanced Scorecard (BSC).

How would employees in the managerial grades, unions and associations feel about such promises? It was hardly surprising that the majority of them, whose views I sought, were sceptical about such promises and henceforth success of the PMS project. Suffice to say, as at end of 2006; PMS and its much-touted linkages to the reward and recognition system remained a promise.

As you can see, frequent changes of the guards within AFX have created multiple impacts on the change programs and PMS project outcome. Changes to every corner of the business are becoming more extensive yet AFX is still suffering from operational losses. To cap it all, AFX is still without a proper performance management system.

In my opinion, AFX is in a *'state of discontinuity'*. Changes at the helm and introduction of contaminated *"fresh blood"* resulted in *breakages* in the overall change continuum. Newly constructed change programs and projects have failed to bring about the desired results. Faced with poor operating results and poor PMS project outcomes, the spirit of goodwill and trust that once filled the air has now disappeared.

Program and project managers were continuously trapped between the boardroom and the project rooms. On one side, is the board and management team that demanded for an effective and efficient PMS implementation; while the other side, are groups that have lost their faith in the PMS initiatives.

Over a period of 24 years (1982-2006) and despite the fact that, PMS is both a technically and financially viable project, it had yet to realise the _real_ benefits for AFX. Perceptions by the masses within AFX pointed to the fact that the whole PMS initiative was not managed vigilantly.

Similar to PMS and other major projects within AFX, the changing of the guards and project ownerships had resulted in consequential changes to the project plans and the overall program as a whole. Unwilling to fully comprehend the history, every newly formed management team started to reinvent programs with new projects, claiming that previous change programs lacked the critical ingredient for success. Although, there were some elements of truth in such a statement, not learning from history is causing AFX to repeat the same mistakes once too often.

Although timing is critical in any change program and projects, sufficient "space" must be given to both management team and employees to manoeuvre the program and projects. Basing on the change trends and history of AFX, lack of such provision had contributed to these successive failures.

These transformations (change programs) have also created mutation of cultures resulting in the assimilation of individuals into the mutated culture, beliefs or disbeliefs and finally, annihilation of caring employees.

These *mutations, assimilations, and annihilations* have killed many programs and projects that are considered not politically correct, even though they were both technically sound and financially viable.

Unlike my cooking concoctions, AFX is NOT something that you throw into the trash compactor! However, continuous tweaking of a misguided programs and projects (like my earlier cited 'foul dish') does not make it any better either; especially when these individuals or groups that came from differing industries, which suffers from "DOPer" Syndrome were oblivious to the surrounding and refusing to learn from history.

Since, every change program and projects ended in *"the circus of project failures"*, AFX is stuck in an irreversible fall!

CLOSING REMARKS:
There is never anything to conclude

I seldom use the word conclusion as there is nothing conclusive, and there is never anything to conclude in the world of project realities. It may be yesterday, today, or tomorrow, the fact remains, program and project managers are constantly trapped within such realities.

When projects within the total programs were not up to the expectations, project management is frequently put to blame. *Denial* of project realities and *insufficient* emphasis on project success factors has led to multiple project failures. In the quest for success, the field of project management is never short of critical success factors advocated by various authors and practitioners.

Discussions held with project owners and team members have led to the discovery of *management support* as the most *critical* success factor, and *project politics* or more safely termed as *project visibility* as a *key* success factor that has a significant influence on both management support and project success. Hence, orchestrating the interplay between the project's internal and external influences is crucial in sustaining and achieving the desired outcome.

Despite presentations and seminars run by the experts, these realities on managing projects are merely acknowledged at a very superficial level, rather than internalised and practised. The rhetoric about how and why the need for change was not seen physically translated into actions and behaviours.

Although financial and technical viability were used as the main parameters in decision-making, the political viability of projects remained prominent and yet were least discussed. This book has surfaced its related *implications* to any program or project managers, in any organisations. Let us re-evaluate our positions before engaging ourselves in the next battle.

The "*circus of project failures*" is being performed everywhere worldwide. The concept of management by blaming others (MBBO) is predominant, and many organisations are facing a *unique* situation. On the one hand, project teams are of the opinion that management support is critical for project success, while on the other hand the management team (board inclusive) and owners feel that project management competency is critical for success. It is always something or someone to take the blame except oneself. However, both parties agree that *management support* does affect project success with only the intensity varying.

It is imperative for program and project managers in any organisation to take the necessary efforts in rationalising and consolidating these factors that are causing or influencing these opinions in moving projects forward. This will put an end to "*the circus of project failures*".

Considering the change history of AFX, MDs may come and goes but what is left behind are the contaminated "*fresh blood*", the *mutation* of cultures, beliefs or disbeliefs; the *assimilation* of the masses and the *annihilation* of the "*wise-ones*"; with program and project managers trapped in between!

A comprehensive understanding on the issues at hand will help to mitigate the risk of project failures. We have briefly described, how easy it is for the "*fresh blood*" be contaminated with impurities that suffer from "*DOPer*" Syndrome, get into the organisational grid. Preconceived wrongful opinions and prejudices do not help anyone. More often than not, such behaviours had created a backlash; and will hit without us even knowing it. Undermining the capabilities of any group or individual does not work to our advantage.

It is normal to have groups that support or work against any change programs and projects. Those that were silent may not necessarily be true supporters and likewise, those "*brave-souls*" may not necessarily be fully against. Sometimes, these "*brave-souls*" can be the best defence any program and project managers could ever have. There is a need to carefully identify the appropriate personalities to avoid disappointments.

It is said that history tends to repeat itself. Therefore, learning the experiences gathered from past programs and projects can help in producing better change program designs and project implementation.

It is also normal for any individual or group to resist new learning. However, for effective learning to take place, the unlearning process has to occur first. *Do not be afraid to unlearn.* There is a need for program and project managers to understand and learn *not* only from what went wrong, but from what was done right is also important. Hiding one's ignorance by being arrogant will not take anyone anywhere!

Project Management is not something that can be learnt within one module in one semester, but rather it is a life-long learning experience. Although these modules provide a basic understanding of project management processes, it focuses more on the hard issues rather than the soft skills in managing people. Project management is a *horizontal* competency that cuts across the whole spectrum of the business, where managing people and human relationships are fundamental. It is therefore imperative that more emphasis be given to this area of *managing people.* I believe this is something that has been mentioned all too often in many presentations, seminars and publications, but in reality actions and behaviours often reflects otherwise. If people are its most important asset a company could ever have, start treating them like one!

A structured Program and Project Management development program for both management and project team members will help in building a cohesive team and sustaining such competency within the organisation, should we honestly want to affect change.

There is a need for organisations to align all project undertakings in a more defined project *'fit'* within the overall corporate strategy and business objectives. The governance, the measure of success, and its impact on the overall performance of the company, are different for different project groups. Regardless of the company's core business, putting in place an effective and efficient project management system is equally important. A proper measurement system for all projects will provide companies with standardised and uniformed measures for current and future projects. This will enable a proper *verdict* to be given to projects; whether it is successful or otherwise.

Realistic targets must be set, with sufficient time given for all excellent projects within the programs to grow and improve as they progress. Seeding excellent projects is like rice planting in a paddy field. Changes in the climate and attacks from pests do affect the crop's output and quality. Hence, it takes plenty of caring, time, and effort to ensure an excellent yield for harvesting.

Similar with earlier cited PMS projects, regardless of changes at the helm and changes in names, the project must be allowed to grow and mature. It is easy for us to dismantle old projects and it is also easy to launch any new program without much consideration to history. However, we need to bear in mind that, the consequences of such action and behaviour can be more detrimental than beneficial. Politically manoeuvring key projects such as PMS can be challenging. Loss of trust, confidence, and commitment from the people at large, need far greater recovery plan and is wasteful on resources. It requires great care, time, and effort in order to reap the full benefits of the PMS project.

Program and Project Managers are constantly trapped.

They are trapped between the needs and expectations of management (board inclusive) and other project's stakeholders. Pressured by the changing business environment and coupled with the subjective nature of the human mind, these needs and expectations do change from time to time. Regardless of change programs and projects, please remember that, it is not those fancy business models or wild jargon that we used but it is the _people_ that make or break a company. As long as it meets the desired project outcomes, keeping things simple but structured may win more followers and supporters for the programs and the projects.

Balancing the technical and financial viabilities is hard enough, but adding the project's political realities can make any project manager delusional.

These are the _realities_ of the project world!

~END~

Below is an extract of the hypothesis testing used in my Doctoral thesis for your consumption:

When modelled together[20], the correlation coefficient (R) is 0.875, indicating both project visibility [PV] and top management support [MS] is positive and strongly related to project success [PS] (*PV, MS* to *PS*; $r = 0.875$, $p< 0.001$). The adjusted variance is 0.744 indicating that 74.4% of project success is explained by both project visibility and top management support (adjusted *PV, MS* to *PS*; $r^2 = 0.744$, $p< 0.001$). These findings are significant and highly unlikely that it has risen by sampling error (*PV, MS* to *PS*; $F=34.432$, $df=2,21$, $p< 0.001$).

Model Summary[b]

Model	R	R Square	Adjusted R Square	Std. Error of the Estimate	R Square Change	Change Statistics			
						F Change	df1	df2	Sig. F Change
1	.875[a]	.766	.744	5.766781	.766	34.432	2	21	.000

a. Predictors: (Constant), Visibility computed mean score (PV), Management Support computed mean score (MS_c)

b. Dependent Variable: Project Success mean score (PS)

ANOVA[b]

Model		Sum of Squares	df	Mean Square	F	Sig.
1	Regression	2290.109	2	1145.054	34.432	.000[a]
	Residual	698.371	21	33.256		
	Total	2988.480	23			

a. Predictors: (Constant), Visibility computed mean score (PV), Management Support computed mean score (MS_c)

b. Dependent Variable: Project Success mean score (PS)

[20] Analysis was done using the input of 578 project team members and 70 project owners who participated in the 24 selected major projects from 1988-2004. The project visibility (PV) mean is 9.05137, top management support (MS) mean is 156.81529, and project success (PV) mean is 66.25767. The Pearson's correlation of PV to PS is 0.760, MS to PS is 0.875, and PV to MS is 0.853.

BIBLIOGRAPHY

Listed below are references that were made in writing this book. Although some may have not been directly cited in the text, they were referred to and it would be unjust not to mention them for their knowledge and contributions.

A guide to project management body of knowledge (PMBOK®). (1996 ed.); (2000 ed.). Newton Square, Pennsylvania, USA: Project Management Institute (PMI).

Adizes, I. (1988). Corporate lifecycles: how and why corporations grow and die and what to do about it. Englewood Cliffs, New Jersey: Prentice Hall.

Ahmad Faisal. (1990). Qwiknet professional advance course and PSDI Australia clients visits Report. Dated 7th December 1990. Unpublished documents.

_____. (1991). Managing Organisational Change, Project Paper DIMP 66/003. Kuala Lumpur, Malaysia: Malaysian Institute of Management.

_____. (1992)(a). Kepner-Tregoe project management workshop report. Dated 15th March 1992. Unpublished documents.

_____. (1992)(b). Information resource planning (IRP) and integrated production planning and control system: QANTAS Australia visit report. Dated 16th May 1992. Unpublished documents.

_____. (1994). Project Management - an introduction, proceedings from American Malaysia Chambers of commerce - young entrepreneurs program, presented on 26th March 1994. Unpublished documents.

_____. (1995). Project Management workshop - Concepts and Applications, proceedings from International Air Transport Association (IATA) - Information Management Conference 1995, presented on 1-5th May 1995. Kuala Lumpur, Malaysia: IATA.

_____. (2001)(a). Beginners' guide to project management. Unpublished documents.

_____. (2001)(b). Project management level 2 workshop guidebook. (3rd ed.). Unpublished documents.

_____. (2004). Project management level 1 workshop guidebook. (6th ed.). Unpublished documents.

Aladwani, M.A. (2002). IT project uncertainty, planning and success: an empirical investigation from Kuwait. Information Technology & People, Vol. 15 No. 3, 2002, pages 210-226. MCB University Press Limited. Retrieved on 25th August 2004 from http://ariel.emeraldinsight.com/vl=1399191/cl=36/nw=1/fm=docpdf/rpsv/cw/mcb/09593845/v15n3/s2/p210.

Allgar, V., Heywood, P., Leese, B. and Walker, R. (2001). First wave PMS pilots: a critical analysis of documentation, Journal of Management in Medicine, Vol.15 No. 4, 2001, pages 299-311. MCB University Press Limited. Retrieved on 20th August 2004 from http://miranda.emeraldinsight.com/vl=11818136/cl=30/nw=1/fm=docpdf/rpsv/cw/mcb/02689235/v15n4/s4/p299

Atkinson, E.P. (1990). Creating cultural change: the keys to successful total quality management. Bedford, UK: IFS Publication Ltd.

Badiru, B.A. and Pulat, S.P. (1995). Comprehensive project management: integrating optimisation models, management principles and computers. Englewood Cliff, New Jersey: Prentice Hall.

Block, R.T. (1999). The seven secrets of a successful project office. PM Network – The professional magazine of Project Management Institute, April 1999 page 4. PMI. Retrieved on 11th March 2004 from http://www.iil.com/members/projectoffice2.asp

Block, R.T and Frame, D.J. (1998). Evolution of project office. Retrieved on 5th July 2004 from http://www.systemcorp.com/en/downloads/block2_r.html

Boudreau, M. and Robey, D. (1996). Coping with contradictions in business process re-engineering. Information Technology & People, Vol.9, No.4, 1996, pages 40-57. MCB University Press Limited. Retrieved on 25th August 2004 from http://iris.emeraldinsight.com/vl=2503617/cl=102/nw=1/fm=docpdf/rpsv/cw/mcb/09593845/v9n4/s3/p40

Bourne, L. and Walker, D. (2004). Advancing project management in learning organisations, The learning organisation Vol. 11 No.3, 2004 pages 226-243. Emerald Group Publishing Limited. Retrieved on 25th August 2004 from http://ariel.emeraldinsight.com/vl=2180091/cl=49/nw=1/fm=docpdf/rpsv/cw/mcb/09696474/v11n3/s3/p226

Brennan, M. (2003). Blended learning and business change: study excerpts and key findings. Retrieved on 8th March 2004 from http://www.lguide.com/blended%20learning%20summary_lg.pdf.

Bryde, J.D. (2002). Modelling project management performance. International journal of quality and reliability management Vol. 20, No. 2, 2002 pages 229-254. MCB University Press limited. Retrieved on 30th October 2004 from http://caliban.emeraldinsight.com/vl=946739/cl=13/nw=1/rpsv/cgi-bin/linker?reqidx=/cw/mcb/09685227/v7n1/s2/p23.idx&lkey=-682565762&rkey=407706.

Bryde, J.D. (2003). Project management concepts, methods and application. International journal of operations and production management Vol. 23, No. 7, 2003 pages 775-793. MCB University Press Limited. Retrieved on 25th August 2004 from http://iris.emeraldinsight.com/vl=1303322/cl=80/nw=1/fm=docpdf/rpsv/cw/mcb/01443577/v23n7/s4/p775

Carnall, C. (1991). Managing change. London: Routledge.

Cicmil, J.K.S. (1997). Critical factors of effective project management. The TQM magazine, Vol. 9, No. 6, 1997 pages 390-396. MCB University Press Limited. Retrieved on 22nd July 2004 from http://ceres.emeraldinsight.com/vl=1805439/cl=47/nw=1/fm=docpdf/rpsv/cw/mcb/0954478x/v9n6/s2/p390

Cicmil, S. (1999). An insight into management of organisational change projects. Journal of Workplace Learning, Vol.11 No.1,1999, pages 5-16. MCB University Press Limited. Retrieved on 25th August 2004 from http://iris.emeraldinsight.com/vl=2247589/cl=73/nw=1/fm=docpdf/rpsv/cw/mcb/13665626/v11n1/s1/p5

Cicmil, S. (2000). Quality in project environments: a non-conventional agenda. International Journal of Quality & Reliability Management, Vol. 17 Nos. 4/5, 2000, pages 554-570. MCB University Press Limited. Retrieved on 25th August 2004 from http://caliban.emeraldinsight.com/vl=2170481/cl=17/nw=1/fm=docpdf/rpsv/cw/mcb/0265671x/v17n4/s15/p554

Chu, J. (1997). Hydro-Electric Corporation's PMLink: a case study of re-engineering through workflow computing. Business Process Management Journal, Vol3. No.2, 1997, pages 162-172. MCB University Press Limited. Retrieved on 20th August 2004 from http://miranda.emeraldinsight.com/vl=11778256/cl=30/nw=1/fm=docpdf/rpsv/cw/mcb/14637154/v3n2/s4/p162

Cleland, I. D. and King R.W. (1983). System analysis and project management (3rd edition). Singapore: McGraw Hill International.

_____ (editors). (1988). Project management handbook (2nd edition). New York: John Wiley & Sons Inc.

Covey, R. S. (1990). The 7 habits of highly effective people. New York: Fireside-Simon & Schuster Inc.

_____, Merill, A.R. and Merill, R.R. (1994). First things first. New York: Simon & Schuster Inc.

Craig, L.R. (1996). The ASTD training and development handbook: a guide to human resources development (4th ed.). New York: McGraw Hill Inc.

Dancey, P.C and Reidy, J. (2002). Statistics without maths for psychology – using SPSS for window (2nd edition). England: Prentice Hall.

David, W. (1987). The innovators - the essential guide to business thinkers, achievers and entrepreneurs. London: Ebury Press Ltd.

Davis, K. (1987). Human behaviour at work - organisational behaviour. New York: McGraw Hill Inc.

Davison, R and Martinsons, M. (2002). Empowerment or enslavement? A case of process-based organisational change in Hong Kong. Information Technology and People, Vol.15 No.1, 2002, pages 42-59. MCB University Press Limited. Retrieved on 25th August 2004 from http://ceres.emeraldinsight.com/vl=5677736/cl=17/nw=1/fm=docpdf/rpsv/cw/mcb/09593845/v15n1/s3/p42

DeBono, E. (1989). Tactics- the art & science of success. London: Fontana.

Drew, S. (1996). Accelerating change: financial industry experience with business process reengineering. International journal of bank marketing, No. 14 Vol. 6, 1996, pages 23-25. MCB University Press Limited. Retrieved on 25th August 2004 from http://miranda.emeraldinsight.com/vl=792821/cl=55/nw=1/fm=docpdf/rpsv/cw/mcb/02652323/v14n6/s3/p23

Drucker, F. P. (1988). Management: task, responsibilities, practices. London: Heinemann Professional Publishing Ltd.

Edwards, M. and Ewen, A. (1996). 360-degrees feedback: royal fail or holy grail? Career Development International, Vol.1, No.3, 1996, pages 28-31. MCB University Press Limited. Retrieved on 25th August 2004 from http://ariel.emeraldinsight.com/vl=2602386/cl=38/nw=1/fm=docpdf/rpsv/cw/mcb/13620436/v1n3/s6/p28

Gould, M. and Freeman, R. (n.d). The art of project management: a competency model for project managers. Retrieved on 15th March 2004 from http://www.butrain.com/pdf/MDPArtofProjectManagement.pdf

Green, G. (2002). Training and development. Oxford, UK: Capstone Publishing (A Wiley company).

Groberg and Riskas, T. (n.d.). Leadership empowerment – turning resistance into commitment, seven habits of highly effective people Seminar on 22nd – 24th March 1994; Kuala Lumpur: Covey Leadership Centre.

Grundy, T and Brown, L. (2003). Developing the individual. Oxford, UK: Capstone Publishing (A Wiley company).

Hacker, M. and Washington, M. (2004). How do we measure the implementation of large scale change? Measuring business excellence, Vol.8, No.3, 2004. pages 52-59. Emerald Group Publishing Limited. Retrieved on 30th October 2004 from http://titania.emeraldinsight.com/vl=5820368/cl=29/nw=1/fm=docpdf/rpsv/cw/mcb/13683047/v8n3/s6/p52.

Haikonen, A., Savolainen, T. and Ja¨rvinen, P. (2003). Exploring six sigma and CI capability development: preliminary case study findings on management role. Journal of Manufacturing Technology Management, Vol. 15, No.4, 2004. pages 369-378. Emerald Group Publishing Limited. Retrieved on 25th August 2004 from http://ceres.emeraldinsight.com/vl=5335298/cl=46/nw=1/fm=docpdf/rpsv/cw/mcb/1741038x/v15n4/s7/p369

Handy, C. (1987). Understanding organisation. London: Penguin Business Library.
_____. (1990). Inside organisation. London: British Broadcasting Corp. Books.

How BPR oiled Mobil's wheels in Australia: a world of change. Human Resources Management International Digest, Vol.11 No.2, 2003, pages 27-29. MCB University Press Limited. Retrieved on 25th August 2004 from http://ceres.emeraldinsight.com/vl=5677736/cl=17/nw=1/fm=html/rpsv/cw/mcb/09670734/v11n2/s7/p27

How project management keeps Sun shining: the consequence of effective prioritisation, Strategic Direction, Vol.20 No.8, 2004, pages 30-32. Emerald Group Publishing Limited. Retrieved on 20th August 2004 from http://caliban.emeraldinsight.com/vl=2348195/cl=44/nw=1/fm=docpdf/rpsv/cw/mcb/02580543/v20n8/s8/p30

Henderson, J and McAdam, R. (2000). Managing quality in project-based emerging network organisations. International Journal of Quality and Reliability Management, Vol.17 No.4/5, 2000, pages 364-376. MCB University Press Limited. Retrieved on 20th August 2004 from http://caliban.emeraldinsight.com/vl=3816923/cl=31/nw=1/fm=docpdf/rpsv/cw/mcb/0265671x/v17n4/s2/p364

Herzog, V. (2001). Trust building on corporate collaborative project teams. Project Management Journal, Vol.31 No. 1, March 2001, pages 28-37. PMI.

Hides, M.T. and Irani, Z. (2000). Facilitating total quality through effective project management. International Journal of Quality and Reliability Management, Vol.17 No.4/5, 2000, pages 207-422. MCB University Press. Retrieved on 25th August 2004 from http://iris.emeraldinsight.com/vl=2503617/cl=102/nw=1/fm=docpdf/rpsv/cw/mcb/0265671x/v17n4/s5/p407

Ilersic, A.R. and Pluck, R.A. (1979). Statistics (14th Edition). London: HFL (Publishers) Ltd.

Imai, M. (1991). Ky'zen - the keys to Japan's competitive success. Singapore: McGraw Hill International.

Ishikawa, K. (1985). What is total quality control-the Japanese way. Englewood Cliffs, New Jersey: Prentice hall Inc.

Jiang, J., Klien, G., Chen, H. (2001). The relative influence of IS project implementation policies and project leadership on eventual outcomes. Project Management Journal, Vol.32 No.3, September 2001, pages 49-55. PMI.

Kaplan S.R. and Norton P.D. (2004). Strategy maps: converting intangible assets into tangible outcomes - a summary, SAS Institute. Retrieved on 21st December 2005 from http://www.sas.com/solutions/spm/StrategyMaps.pdf

Kerzner, H. (1990). Project management for bankers, New York: Van Nostrand Reinhold.

_____ (1992). Project management - a system approach to planning, scheduling and control (4th ed.). New York: Van Nostrand Reinhold.

Kuruppuarachchi, R.P., Mandal, P. and Smith, R. (2002). IT project implementation strategies for effective changes: a critical review. Logistics Information Management, Vol. 15, No. 2, 2002. pages 126-137. MCB University Press Limited. Retrieved on 22nd July 2004 from http://ceres.emeraldinsight.com/vl=1777606/cl=83/nw=1/fm=docpdf/rpsv/cw/mcb/09576053/v15n2/s5/p126

Lee-Kelly, L. (2002). Situational leadership: managing the virtual project team, Journal of Management Development, Vol.21 No.6, 2002, pages 461-476. MCB University Press Limited. Retrieved on 25th August 2004 from http://iris.emeraldinsight.com/vl=1303322/cl=80/nw=1/fm=docpdf/rpsv/cw/mcb/02621711/v21n6/s4/p461

Loo, R. (1996). Training in project management: a powerful tool for improving individual and team performance. Team Performance Management: An International Journal, Vol.12 No.3, 1996, pages 6-14. MCB University Press Limited. Retrieved on 25th August 2005 from http://iris.emeraldinsight.com/vl=1601522/cl=77/nw=1/fm=docpdf/rpsv/cw/mcb/13527592/v2n3/s1/p6

Luthans, F. (1989). Organisational behaviour. Singapore: McGraw Hill International.

Morris, W.G.P. (2001). Updating the project management bodies of knowledge. Project Management Journal vol.32 no.3, September 2001, pages 21-30. PMI.

Nemati, R.H. and Barko, D. C. (2003) Key factors for achieving organizational data-mining success. Industrial Management & Data Systems Vol. 103 No. 4, 2003, pages 282-292. MCB University Press Limited. Retrieved on 20th August 2004 from http://miranda.emeraldinsight.com/vl=11778256/cl=30/nw=1/fm=docpdf/rpsv/cw/mcb/02635577/v103n4/s7/p282.

Nirmul G. A and Rigatuso G. (2004). White Paper: Strategy-focused business planning – to create sustained corporate performance. Balanced Scorecard Collaborative, Inc. Retrieved on 21st December 2005 from http://www.oracle.com/applications/financials/SFBP_whitepaper.pdf

O'hare, M. (1988). Innovate! - how to gain and sustain competitive advantages. Oxford: Basil Blackwell Ltd.

Obeng, E. and Crainer, S. (1996). What's wrong with organisation anyway? Making re-engineering happen. London: FT Pitman Publishing.

Ohmae, K. (1988). The mind of the strategist. Middlesex, England: Penguin Books Ltd.

_____. (1991). The borderless world – power and strategy in the interlinked economy. London: Fontana-Harper Collins.

Oldenboom, N. and Abratt, R. (2000). Success and failure in developing new banking and insurance services in South Africa. International Journal of Bank Marketing, Vol.18, No.5, 2000, pages 233-245. Retrieved on 25th August 2004 from http://miranda.emeraldinsight.com/vl=792821/cl=55/nw=1/fm=docpdf/rpsv/cw/mcb/02652323/v18n5/s3/p233

Peter, T. (1989). Thriving on chaos. London: Pan Books Macmillan.

Peters, J. (editor). (1987). Action for change: the politics of implementation. MCB university journal, vol.8 no.4. 1987 pages 17-87. MCB University Press limited: Bradford, England.

Pitagorsky, G. (n.d.). Implementing PM improvement- a cultural and organisational change initiative. Retrieved on 11th March 2004 from http://www.iil.com/members/implementing2.asp

Prasad, B. (1995). A structured approach to product and process optimisation for manufacturing and service industries, International Journal of Quality and Reliability Management, Vol.12 No.9, 1995, pages 123-138. MCB University Press Limited. Retrieved on 20th August 2004 from http://ariel.emeraldinsight.com/vl=583614/cl=18/nw=1/fm=docpdf/rpsv/cw/mcb/0265671x/v12n9/s8/p123

Programme Management Survey. (n.d.). KPMG Consulting Group. Retrieved on 5th January 2004 from http://www.kpmg.co.uk/pubs/risk_survey.pdf.

Project Management gives BAT a boost, Human Resource Management, Vol.12 No.1, 2004, pages 21-23. Emerald Group Publishing Limited. Retrieved on 20th August 2004 from http://iris.emeraldinsight.com/vl=11728087/cl=33/nw=1/fm=docpdf/rpsv/cw/mcb/09670734/v12n1/s7/p21

Rashid, A.Z.M., Sambasivan, M. and Rahman, A.A. (2004). The influence of organisational culture on attitudes towards organisational change. The leadership and Organisation Development Journal, Vol.25 No.2, 2004, pages 161-179. Emerald Publishing Limited. Retrieved on 25th August 2004 from http://haly.emeraldinsight.com/vl=2949157/cl=56/nw=1/fm=docpdf/rpsv/cw/mcb/01437739/v25n2/s3/p161

Robbins-Gioia Inc. (n.d). White Paper: A guide to successful project management. Retrieved on 10th March 2004 from http://www.robbinsgioia.com/library/whitepapers/WP~Guide2ProjSuccess.pdf

Robbins-Gioia Inc. (2002). White paper: ten critical steps for successful project portfolio management. Retrieved on 10th March 2004 from http://www.robbinsgioia.com/library/whitepapers/WP~PFM10Steps.pdf.

Rolls-Royce a driving force in project management: mind the gap, Human Resource Management International Digest, Vol.11 No.6, 2003, pages 26-28. MCB University Press Limited. Retrieved on 21st August 2004 from http://ceres.emeraldinsight.com/vl=5221264/cl=27/nw=1/rpsv/cgi-bin/userpassreq?/cw/mcb/09670734/v11n6/s7/p26

Rue, W. L. and Holland, G. P. (1989). Strategic management – concepts and experiences (2nd ed.). Singapore: McGraw-Hill Book Co.

Seely, A.M and Duong, P. Q. (2001). The dynamic baseline model for project management. Project Management Journal vol.32 no.2, June 2001, pages 25-36. PMI.

Sekaran, U. (2003). Research methods for business (4th edition). New York: John Wiley & Sons Inc.

Sivakumar, K. and Nakata, C. (2003). Designing global new product teams: optimising the effects of national culture on new product development. International Marketing Review, Vol.20 No.4, 2003, pages 397-445. MCB University Press Limited. Retrieved on 25th August 2004 from http://miranda.emeraldinsight.com/vl=890122/cl=15/nw=1/fm=docpdf/rpsv/cw/mcb/02651335/v20n4/s4/p397

Smith, M. (2003). Changing an organisation's culture: correlates of success and failure. Leadership and Organisation Development Journal, Vol.24, No.5, 2003, pages 249-261. MCB University Press Limited. Retrieved on 25th August 2004 from http://iris.emeraldinsight.com/vl=2247589/cl=73/nw=1/fm=docpdf/rpsv/cw/mcb/01437739/v24n5/s1/p249

Smith, B and Dodds, B. (2001). Project based learning for developing managers. India: Infinity Books

Sotiriou, D and Wittmer, D. (2001). Influence method of project managers, perception of team members and project managers. Project Management Journal, Vol.32 No.3, September 2001, pages 12-20. PMI.

Stebbins, M., Shani, A., Moon, W. and Bowles, D. (1998). Business process reengineering at Blue Shield of California: the integration of multiple change initiatives. Journal of organisational change management, Vol.11 No.3, 1998, pages 216-232. MCB University Press Limited. Retrieved on 25th August 2004 from http://miranda.emeraldinsight.com/vl=890122/cl=15/nw=1/fm=docpdf/rpsv/cw/mcb/09534814/v11n3/s2/p216

Stewart, E.W (2001). Balances Scorecard for Projects. Project Management Journal vol.32 no.1, March 2001, pages 38-53. PMI.

Strehl, F. and Hugh, U. (1997). Administrative reform in Austria: public administration management as an organisational development process. International journal of public sector management, Vol.10, No.3, 1997, pages 228-239. MCB University Press Limited. Retrieved on 25th August 2004 from http://miranda.emeraldinsight.com/vl=792821/cl=55/nw=1/fm=docpdf/rpsv/cw/mcb/09513558/v10n3/s6/p228

Suomala, P. and Jokioinen, I. (2003), The pattern of success in product development: a case study. European journal of innovation management, Vol.6 No.4, (2003) pages 213-227. MCB University Press Limited. Retrieved on 30th October 2004 from http://puck.emeraldinsight.com/vl=14160487/cl=54/nw=1/fm=docpdf/rpsv/cw/mcb/14601060/v6n4/s2/p213

The CHAOS Report. (1995). Retrieved on 5th March 2004 from http://www.standishgroup.com/sample_research/PDFpages/chaos1994.pdf

The CHAOS : Recipe for success. (1999). Retrieved on 5th March 2004 from http://www.standishgroup.com/sample_research/PDFpages/chaos1999.pdf

The Extreme CHAOS. (2001). Retrieved on 5th March 2004 from http://www.standishgroup.com/sample_research/PDFpages/extreme_chaos.pdf

Thite, M. (1999). Identifying key characteristics of technical project leadership. Leadership & Organization Development Journal, Vol. 20 No.5, 1999 pages 253-261. MCB University Press Limited. Retrieved on 22nd July 2004 from http://ceres.emeraldinsight.com/vl=2897192/cl=111/nw=1/fm=docpdf/rpsv/cw/mcb/01437739/v20n5/s3/p253

Transforming Boeing: enterprise project management in action, Human Resource Management International Digest, Vol.11 No.6, 2003, pages 29-31. MCB University Press Limited. Retrieved on 21st August 2004 from http://miranda.emeraldinsight.com/vl=3326594/cl=69/nw=1/rpsv/~1333/v11n6/s8/p29

Tukel, I.O. and Rom, O.W. (2001). An empirical investigation of project evaluation criteria. International Journal of Operations & Production Management, Vol. 21 No. 3, 2001, pages 400-416. MCB University Press Limited. Retrieved on 21st July 2004 from http://ariel.emeraldinsight.com/vl=833053/cl=33/nw=1/fm=docpdf/rpsv/cw/mcb/01443577/v21n3/s6/p400.

Welman, J.C. and Kruger S.J. (1999). Research methodology for the business and administrative sciences. Southern Africa: Oxford University Press.

Whittaker, B. (1999). What went wrong? Unsuccessful information technology projects. Information Management and Computer Security, Vol.7 No.1, 1999, pages 23-29. MCB University Press Limited. Retrieved on 21st July 2004 from http://caliban.emeraldinsight.com/vl=946739/cl=13/nw=1/rpsv/cgi-bin/linker?reqidx=/cw/mcb/09685227/v7n1/s2/p23.idx&lkey=-682565762&rkey=407706

Zeiberg, C. (2001). Ten steps to successfully selecting a learning management system. Received on 9th March 2004 via email from info@lguide.com requested made from http://www.lguide.com.

Zhang, Q. and Doll, W. (2001). The fuzzy front end and success of new product development: a causal model. European Journal of Innovation Management, Vol.4 No.2, 2001, pages 95-112. MCB University Press Limited. Retrieved on 25th August from http://miranda.emeraldinsight.com/vl=875349/cl=11/nw=1/fm=docpdf/rpsv/cw/mcb/14601060/v4n2/s4/p95